# FULL EMPLOYMENT

# FULL EMPLOYMENT

## IS IT POSSIBLE?

by

Peter M. Rinaldo

DorPete Press     Briarcliff Manor, New York

Copyright © 1994 by DorPete Press
Printed in the United States of America

FIRST EDITION

Library of Congress Catalog
Card Number 94-070583

Grateful acknowledgement is made to Warner/Chappell Music, Inc. for permission to use a portion of the lyrics of "Are You Having Any Fun?" (Sammy Fain, Jack Yellen), Copyright © 1939 by CHAPPELL & CO. (Renewed).

Publisher's Cataloging in Publication
*(Prepared by Quality Books Inc.)*

Rinaldo, Peter M. (Peter Merritt), 1922-
   Full employment : is it possible? / by Peter M. Rinaldo.
   p. cm.
   Includes bibliographical references and index.
   Preassigned LCCN: 94-070583.
   ISBN 0-9622123-8-5

   1. Full employment policies--United States. 2. United States--Economic policy--1993- 3. Labor supply--United States. 4. Hours of labor, Flexible. I. Title.

HC106.8.R56 1989        331.1'1'0973
                                  QBI94-633

# CONTENTS

| | | |
|---|---|---|
| Chapter I | INTRODUCTION:<br>The Need for Full Employment | 1 |
| Chapter II | EMPLOYMENT IN MANUFACTURING:<br>The Missing 7 Million Jobs | 12 |
| Chapter III | EMPLOYMENT IN SERVICES:<br>Physicians, Beauticians,<br>and Auto Technicians | 25 |
| Chapter IV | EMPLOYMENT FROM TECHNOLOGY:<br>From the Space Station to<br>Virtual Reality | 35 |
| Chapter V | EMPLOYMENT FROM STRUCTURE<br>AND INFRASTRUCTURE:<br>Low-Cost Housing and Maglev<br>Trains | 42 |
| Chapter VI | EMPLOYMENT IN GOVERNMENT:<br>Teachers and Bureaucrats | 48 |
| Chapter VII | EMPLOYMENT FROM CREATIVITY:<br>The Arts | 52 |
| Chapter VIII | RECAPITULATION:<br>The Shortage of Jobs | 56 |
| Chapter IX | EMPLOYMENT EFFECTS OF<br>LIMITING YEARS OF WORK:<br>Youth Corps and the Golden Years | 63 |
| Chapter X | EMPLOYMENT EFFECTS OF<br>LIMITING HOURS OF WORK:<br>The Five-Day Weekend<br>Revisited | 69 |

| Chapter XI | CONQUERING THE FEAR OF LEISURE | 75 |
| Chapter XII | FIRST PRECONDITION FOR FULL EMPLOYMENT: An Educated Work Force | 79 |
| Chapter XIII | SECOND PRECONDITION FOR FULL EMPLOYMENT: A Sound Economy | 85 |
| Chapter XIV | THE GREAT GOD GNP | 94 |
| Chapter XV | RECOMMENDATIONS AND CONCLUSIONS | 101 |
| APPENDIX A | EMPLOYMENT AND INFLATION | 107 |
| SOURCES AND NOTES | | 113 |
| INDEX | | 125 |

# ACKNOWLEDGEMENTS

In writing this book, I am more than usually indebted to my family. The idea for the subject came from my wife Dorothy, who has long been concerned that eliminating unemployment did not seem to have a high priority on the national agenda. Subsequently the book benefitted greatly from discussions with two economists named David—my son David Rinaldo, whose Doctorate in Economics is from the University of Michigan, and my son-in-law David Lee, whose Doctorate in Economics is from the University of Wisconsin. They also reviewed an early draft of the book. Although they probably do not agree with all of my conclusions, they were very helpful in preventing egregious errors.

I am also grateful to my friends Bob Coquillette, John McCall, and Doug Eldridge, who reviewed a preliminary draft of the manuscript and made many helpful suggestions on clarification and emphasis.

My research was facilitated by reference librarians at the New York Public Library and the Ossining Public Library. I particularly appreciate the help of Ruth Schwab and Natalie Fogel, reference librarians at the latter institution.

Finally, the designer, Jan Aiello, responsible for the dust jackets of all of my books, has done her usual outstanding job on this one.

                                        Peter M. Rinaldo
                                        April, 1994

## Chapter I

# INTRODUCTION:

## The Need for Full Employment

For most of mankind's history, it would not have been possible for a substantial portion of the population to have been idle without thereby incurring severe shortages of food and other necessities of life for the whole society. The labor of all was required for the support of all. In eighteenth century America, about 70 percent of the labor force was employed in growing food and textile fibers. At that time, the whole family was effectively in the labor force. Wives labored as hard or harder than their husbands ("Man works from sun to sun, but woman's work is never done!"), and children started doing chores as soon as they were physically able to do so.

In contrast, only about 3 percent of the labor force in the United States today is engaged in agriculture. Another 11 percent are the blue-collar workers that manufacture all of our soft and hard goods, from buttons to bulldozers.[1] Thus, less than 15 percent of the work force, or about 16 million people, grow or make everything we eat or use, excluding imported goods, but including exports. Many, perhaps most, of the readers of this book will not personally know a full-time farmer or a blue-collar manufacturing

# CHAPTER I

worker, in spite of the fact that we ultimately depend on these men and women for both our necessities and our luxuries. Of course, additional people are required to manage and finance the manufacturing companies and to distribute and market these goods, but a substantial portion of the remaining 85 percent of the work force could be unemployed, even at full production of food and manufactured goods, without endangering the supplies of bread or fur coats for the population as a whole.

Nevertheless, for a variety of reasons, most adult Americans want jobs. In the past there have been societies in which work was not highly regarded. In nineteenth-century England, the leisure class looked upon work with contempt. In ancient Greece and the antebellum American South, slaves did manual labor but most free citizens did not. The existence of such societies shows that there probably is no <u>instinctual</u> basis for the desire to work. For the average individual in America today the motivation to work is likely some combination of:

    (a) the psychological needs to be busy and useful;

    (b) the desire for material possessions that work will afford; and

    (c) the social approval that working brings.[2]

This motivation to work is so strong that for most people unemployment is emotionally devastating.

Unemployment also has strong negative effects that contribute to widespread social problems. If people, and especially young people, cannot find jobs and earn a living through productive employment, they choose the alternative of obtaining money through burglary and mugging. Unemployment poses a severe strain on marriage and leads to the breakdown of families, with consequent unfortunate effects on the children.

Thus, full employment is a highly desirable social goal. Further, for our consumer-based economic system to function, income from employment must be sufficiently

Introduction

widespread in the population so that there is a market for the goods and services that are produced. If all or most of the national income is in the hands of the few, as it used to be in feudal societies and is today in some third-world countries, satisfying the needs of the few provides employment for only a small part of the population. The unemployed not only make no productive contribution to society as a whole but also do not provide the taxes that our complex industrial state requires for government services.

Thus, we come back to the question of full employment. At this point, we shall attempt to define what "full employment" means. The Bureau of Labor Statistics (BLS) of the U.S. Department of Labor calculates a number of different unemployment rates using different sets of criteria. The measure usually reported in the media, which the BLS designates as U-5, does not consider those who have become discouraged about finding a job as being unemployed. In this definition, an unemployed person must be actively seeking a job. The Bureau does, however, make a separate estimate of how many people want a job but for various reasons, such as being discouraged, are not looking for one. In 1992, when the total labor force was 128 million, the Bureau reported that the number of workers who wanted a job but were not looking for one was 6.2 million.[3] It also reported that about 19 million people were working in part-time jobs, of whom 4.4 million would like to work full time. Neither these involuntary part timers nor the discouraged job seekers were considered in the usual (U-5) reported statistics as being part of the ranks of the "unemployed."[4]

Apart from the BLS statisticians, though, most people would consider full employment as a condition that exists when there is a full-time job outside the home for anyone who desires it. There always will be a small percent of the work force at any one time that is in the process of changing from one job to another, so the maximum employment rate

3

## CHAPTER I

can never be 100 percent. Both Sweden and Japan, however, have shown that it is possible to function successfully for twenty years or more with an employment rate of at least 97 percent.[5] This book will accept their experience and define full employment as a condition in which those who are working full time are at least 97 percent of those eligible persons who want full-time jobs.

The reader will notice that the restrictive word "eligible" was added to the previous sentence. Many thirteen- and fourteen-year-old children would now like to work in order to have the money to buy several fancy jackets and more pairs of shoes, but under current child labor laws they are not eligible for employment. As we examine the problem of achieving full employment, we shall consider the possibility of adding other restrictions on who is eligible to work. For the purposes of this book, those not in the eligibility pool will not be considered unemployed.

Of course, the definition of a "full-time job" also varies from country to country. In the United States, the current norm in manufacturing is a 40-hour week, with an average of 23 days off per year for vacations and holidays. In contrast, the average full-time German manufacturing worker spends only 37.6 hours per week on the job and has 42 days off for vacations and holidays. After adding in other days away from the job for reasons such as paid sick leave and paid child-care leave, the average full-time German worker spends almost 20 percent fewer hours per year on his or her job than the typical American worker.[6] This book will also consider the option of increasing employment by having each worker spend fewer hours on the job. For instance, if all of the blue-collar manufacturing workers in the United States reduced their working hours to the German average, about 3 million more jobs would be created here. Proposals to share existing work by reducing the working hours of individuals will be explored in a later chapter. If

Introduction

handled properly, this change need not reduce the annual earnings of individuals gaining more free time.

The other restriction in the above definition of full employment is that the term applies only to those who <u>want</u> to work outside the home. Most people would agree that women (and men) who find satisfaction in working in the home to raise their children or simply to keep house should not be considered unemployed. Nor should the millionaire who enjoys being a playboy or the hobo who likes a vagabond life be counted in the unemployed statistics. Neither the millionaire playboy nor the hobo contributes anything to society except, perhaps, to provide local color. The more people, however, who opt out of the labor force, the easier the task of finding jobs for those who do want to work.

How many new full-time jobs will be required to provide employment for 97 percent of those who wish to work full time? In 1992 it would have been about 16 million new slots—5.5 million to bring the unemployment rate down from 7.3 percent to 3 percent (the minimum level of "structural" unemployment), plus 6.2 million who want a job but are not actively seeking one, plus 4.4 million to provide full-time jobs for the part-timers who want to work full time. In this book, we shall focus on the year 2005, since the BLS has made employment estimates for that year based on actual figures for the year 1992. (The BLS estimates, summarized in a series of articles in the November 1993 issue of *Monthly Labor Review*, are used throughout this book.) Its estimate is that the work force will grow by 24 million people between 1992 and 2005.[7] Clearly, to create 40 million new jobs in the thirteen years between 1992 and 2005 is a monumental task.

Many politicians and some economists have suggested that the cure for U.S. unemployment problems is to redress our unfavorable balance of foreign trade. There is no question that the number of jobs in the United States is

5

## CHAPTER I

affected by the level of our imports and exports. We can increase employment by exporting more goods, whereas imported goods provide jobs in other countries, rather than here. According to those espousing the policy of free trade, however, these sources of employment through export and of unemployment through import tend in the long run to balance out. Even when the United States is running a substantial trade deficit in manufactured goods, as is true in the early 1990s, the net job loss in the United States because of this manufacturing trade deficit is probably about 740,000 jobs out of our total labor force of more than 125 million.[8] For the purposes of this book, we shall accept the free-trade thesis and neglect the employment effects of trade policy.

For similar reasons, this book considers only the U.S. economy, rather than the greatly more complex world economy. Of course, what happens in the rest of the world does have an influence on employment in the United States. In some industries, such as automobile manufacturing, a change in the relative value of the yen and the dollar can have a marked effect on sales and employment. It should be noted, however, that the total employment in the automotive industry is less than 800,000, and this figure has fluctuated less than 5 percent over the past fifteen years.[9] The total U.S. work force is more than 125 million, so the automotive industry employment amounts to less than 1 percent of the total. Ups and downs in automotive sales because of foreign exchange variations have little significant effect on total employment. The situation in other industries is similar. The U.S. Gross National Product (GNP) of nearly $5 trillion is so huge (10 to 12 times greater) in relation to either exports of $400 billion or imports of $500 billion that even major fluctuations in exchange rates produce only a minor effect on overall U.S. employment. This is not to say that the United States should not strive to be competitive in world markets, but as far as overall employment is concerned,

Introduction

internal politics are much more significant than external policies.

At this point, it should be mentioned that most U.S. economists believe that it would be impossible to achieve full employment as defined in this book (less than 3 percent unemployed) without at the same time producing an unacceptably high rate of inflation. According to Milton Friedman and others, there is a certain level of unemployment that is consistent with stable prices (or an acceptably low rate of inflation). If the government tries to increase demand to reduce unemployment below this critical level, unacceptably high rates of inflation will result. This critical unemployment rate is termed the "nonaccelerating inflation rate of unemployment" or NAIRU. In the United States in the early 1990s the NAIRU is considered to be between 5 and 7 percent.[10]

Economics, however, is not a "hard" science like physics. None of its laws have the predictive power of the Law of Gravity. In particular, it is often difficult in economics to distinguish between a cause and effect relationship between two factors and a chance correlation. There have been periods in the United States when both inflation and unemployment held at 4 percent or less for a number of years. For instance, for the six years 1948 through 1953, U.S. unemployment averaged 4.0 percent, whereas inflation rose only an average of 2.4 percent.[11] In Japan, both inflation and unemployment have stayed below 3.5 percent for the past five years.[12] In 1992 the cost of living in Japan rose only 1.2 percent in spite of an unemployment rate of only 2.4 percent.[13] Thus, a combination of a low unemployment rate and a low rate of inflation is not only theoretically possible but has been achieved in practice. Those readers who are interested in a further discussion of this question are referred to Appendix A.

Accordingly, we shall proceed on the assumption that full employment is possible without disastrous consequences. Although this book emphasizes the desirability of solving

# CHAPTER I

the unemployment problem through the private sector rather than government employment, the government has an extremely important role to play in establishing two preconditions of full employment. For there to be full employment in this country, there must be an educated work force and the economy itself must be sound. Although full employment is impossible if those desiring jobs do not have the capability of performing satisfactorily in those jobs that are available and although one cannot have full employment in a depressed economy, meeting these preconditions does not guarantee full employment. Thus, these preconditions are <u>necessary</u> but not <u>sufficient</u>. (This phrase comes from science. In chemical experiments, in order for a chemical reaction to take place, certain conditions have to be present. If some, but not all, of these conditions are met, those conditions that are present are referred to as "necessary but not sufficient.")

So assuming a sound economy and an educated work force, there are at least eight different general approaches to increasing employment (The Eightfold Way).

1. <u>Increase the consumption of existing consumer goods</u>, both durable goods such as automobiles and nondurables such as gasoline and galoshes. The factories that produce these goods and the wholesale and retail distribution system that delivers them to the consumer will require more employees. Indirectly, this avenue also leads to more jobs to produce the raw materials and the capital goods required for manufacture of the consumer goods, as well as more jobs in those sectors such as engineering and accounting that service the manufacturing companies. Since the 1930s, Keynesian economists have traditionally focused on this approach.

2. <u>Increase the demand for existing consumer services</u>, which in the broad sense range all the way from hairdressing salons and stock brokerages to symphony orchestras. Supplying this demand will require more employees—

Introduction

more hair stylists, more financial analysts, more violinists, and others.

3. <u>Develop new technologies</u> that will lead to new and different consumer goods and services. The jobs resulting from the development of personal computers, videocassette recorders, and compact disk players have all appeared since World War II.

4. <u>Increase the number of jobs in capital projects</u>, both for building structures such as housing and for the infrastructure such as roads and bridges.

5. <u>Increase the number of employees in government</u> —local, state, and national. This is a broad category that includes teachers and soldiers as well as senators and bureaucrats. It also includes any people funded by guaranteed jobs programs at the various government levels.

6. <u>Increase the number of self-employed artists and writers</u>. Although some artists and writers work for large organizations such as advertising agencies, important contributions to our society are made by those creative people who devote full time to expressing their inner visions.

All of the above approaches involve the creation of more jobs within the present customary hours and years of work. In addition, it is possible to create employment by shortening either or both the number of hours worked per year and the number of years worked in a lifetime:

7. <u>Restrict the eligibility to work at both ends of the age spectrum</u>. Although this does not increase the total number of jobs, it increases the employment opportunities for those who remain eligible.

8. <u>Reduce the standard weekly working hours</u> so that more people are required to do the same amount of work.

# CHAPTER I

The following chapters of this book will explore, in turn, each of the eight methods listed above for increasing employment. The exploration of job-creation possibilities through conventional means in Chapters II through VII will show that the best hope for creating significant numbers of new jobs is to encourage the growth of the service sector. A recapitulation in Chapter VIII will demonstrate how difficult it will be through conventional means to create 40 million new jobs. This chapter will also discuss the possibility of removing some of the employer costs of hiring new employees as well as tilting consumer demand toward the more labor-intensive service sector through changes in taxation. However, since these changes still would not be sufficient to lead to full employment, we shall consider alternatives 7 and 8 above, which involve using more (or different) people to perform existing jobs in the private sector. Because the reforms recommended in this book will result in more leisure time for most of the population, Chapter XI will explore how this leisure might be used and how it will affect the number of jobs through increased consumption of leisure services and products.

The preconditions for full employment mentioned above of an educated work force and a stable and growing economy will be discussed in Chapters XII and XIII. The following chapter will discuss the limitations of using the statistical measurement Gross National Product as the primary gauge of the economic health of the country.

The concluding chapter will consider the possibility of providing full employment by using the government as the employer of last resort. After rejecting this approach for financial and social reasons, the balance of the chapter will summarize which changes in government policies and private sector practices have been recommended in this book in order to bring about full employment. These include such peripheral items as comprehensive testing for educational achievement and the adoption of a universal calendar. They

Introduction

also, however, include two major changes which are sure to be controversial but would have a major effect on employment:

1. Eliminate payroll taxes on salaries below $30,000 per year, adjusting the rates on salaries above that figure (with no upper limit) to produce the same revenue as present taxes. At the same time, adopt a value-added tax (VAT) to replace the present systems of health- care financing for those at the same under-$30,000 salary level. This would encourage private sector employment by reducing the cost of hiring new employees, which should particularly benefit the labor-intensive service sector.

2. Move toward a 35-hour workweek as well as encourage delayed entry into the work force and early retirement. These moves would reduce unemployment by increasing the number of people employed to perform existing jobs.

These two recommendations are interrelated because most of the resistance on the part of employers to reduce the hours in the workweek is caused by the fact that many of their benefit costs, such as health care, are proportional to the number of employees, not to the total number of hours worked.

The final chapter will also include a plea that those governing this country reduce the present overemphasis on the growth of the GNP. Of course, the economy must continue to grow in order for more private-sector jobs to be created. The government, however, should seek to combine overall economic growth with the creation of satisfying jobs for all, the reduction of excessive income disparities, and the protection of the environment. Although this may sound utopian, this book will make a strong case that this is not only possible but necessary.

## Chapter II

# EMPLOYMENT IN MANUFACTURING:

## The Missing 7 Million Jobs

*I*n the United States, personal consumption expenditures for goods and services in 1991 represented about 67 percent of the total U.S. economy (as measured by the National Income and Product accounts compiled by the U.S. Department of Commerce); for goods alone the figure was about 30 percent.[1] Since it seems obvious to most politicians that more consumer goods will mean more jobs, many government policies on job creation have focused on increasing consumer goods production. Investment tax credits have been justified on the basis that increased investment in production machinery to make more consumer goods will lead to more jobs and/or higher productivity. A reduction in the capital gains tax rate is justified on the basis that this incentive will lead to more investment in new enterprises, which will buy new machinery to make new kinds of consumer goods and thus create jobs.

Of course, if one looks at the abundance of goods already in the homes of U.S. consumers, one might ask if there is an insatiable demand for ever-more possessions. From reading the daily newspaper and from discussions with sociologists and economists, the answer seems to be that demand is indeed limitless.

## Employment in Manufacturing

For the great middle class, the desire to "keep up with the Joneses" is strong. Most people are not happy driving a ten-year-old Chevrolet when their neighbor has a new Toyota. Also, Americans are fascinated by the latest gadgets, as is evidenced by the switch from 78 rpm records to 33 rpm LPs to high-fidelity tapes and thence to compact discs. Designs of skis and ski boots change yearly; a skier in the 1990s who still wore boots with laces would be an anomaly. Of course, there were real technical improvements in both the recordings and the boots, but the desire for the latest marvel played a large part in their merchandising, as in the slogan for buckle boots, "Are you still lacing while others are racing?"

In addition to normal and abnormal greed, consumer demand for the latest technological wonders in household appliances and sporting goods, and the desire to keep up with the neighbors, other factors also fuel consumer demand. One is a mania for collecting which I shall call the Imelda Marcos Factor. When the Marcos regime in the Philippines was overthrown in 1986, it was discovered that the president's wife, Imelda Marcos, had more than 3,000 pairs of shoes in her closets. She also had five shelves of Gucci handbags, still with their price tags on, and 68 pairs of gloves.[2] Although this was undoubtedly an extreme case and Imelda Marcos was not an American, lesser examples of the Imelda Marcos Factor can be found in the closets of many of America's homes. The mania for collecting is not confined to clothes. Some specialize in oil paintings; others amass antique dolls, vintage automobiles, or hunting rifles. We are a nation of collectors.

To ensure that our normal acquisitive instincts are not somehow repressed, Americans are subjected to the greatest barrage of advertising for consumer goods that the world has ever known. Much of the mail we receive consists of catalogs for consumer goods from such companies as L.L. Bean and the Banana Republic. Our television and radio

## CHAPTER II

programs are constantly interrupted by inducements to buy General Motors minivans and Rolex watches. Our magazines and newspapers not only have advertisements on the news pages but also contain whole supplements of sales items offered by KMart and J.C. Penney. Then, there are the billboards and neon signs that still pervade our metropolitan areas and, sometimes, even skywriting and blimps in the heavens above.

The effect on consumer spending of this stimulation of consumer demand has been as one might expect. Sales of consumer goods have risen. The following table, adjusted for inflation, shows a twelve-year history of personal consumption expenditures for durable goods such as automobiles and refrigerators and nondurable goods such as soft drinks and textiles, . The third column gives the number of nonsupervisory workers (blue collar) in all manufacturing facilities. This last column is not strictly comparable to the first two since it includes workers in _all_ factories, including those making the capital equipment used in the production of consumer goods. The inclusion of machine tools and other similar sectors, however, should show an even larger employment increase because of the compounding effect.

Employment in Manufacturing

## CONSUMER EXPENDITURES FOR GOODS
(Billions of 1987 Dollars)
## AND FACTORY EMPLOYMENT (Millions)[3]

| YEAR | DURABLE GOODS | NONDURABLE GOODS | FACTORY EMPLOYMENT |
|---|---|---|---|
| 1979 | $289 (Billion) | 863 (Billion) | 15.1 (Million) |
| 1980 | 263 | 861 | 14,2 |
| 1981 | 265 | 868 | 14,1 |
| 1982 | 263 | 873 | 12,7 |
| 1983 | 298 | 900 | 12,5 |
| 1984 | 339 | 935 | 13,3 |
| 1985 | 370 | 959 | 13,1 |
| 1986 | 402 | 991 | 12,9 |
| 1987 | 404 | 1011 | 13,0 |
| 1988 | 429 | 1035 | 13,2 |
| 1989 | 441 | 1049 | 13,3 |
| 1990 | 439 | 1051 | 13,0 |
| 1991 | 413 | 1043 | 12,4 |

Ratio 91/79     1.43           1.21          0.82
Combined Durable and Nondurable: 1.26

The table shows that consumer expenditures, adjusted for inflation, were 43 percent more for durable goods and 21 percent higher for nondurable goods in 1991 than in 1979; the combined growth was 26 percent. Yet, by the end of this twelve-year period, factory employment of blue-collar workers had dropped by 17 percent. If all other factors

15

had stayed constant, the growth (in constant dollars) of 26 percent in demand for consumer goods should have led to a growth of 26 percent in the number of blue-collar workers. These should have grown from 15.1 million in 1979 to more than 19 million in 1991. The actual number of production workers averaged 12.4 million in 1991, dropping to 12.1 million by mid-1993—a <u>decrease</u> of 3 million jobs. Thus, we are missing 7 million workers, the difference between the 19 million expected production workers and the actual 12 million jobs.

The above figures are only for blue-collar production workers. During this twelve-year period, manufacturing companies held their overhead staffs constant at 6 million workers. Thus, total manufacturing employment, including supervisors and supporting staffs, decreased parallel with production-worker employment, dropping by 3 million jobs from 21.0 million workers in 1979 to 18.4 million in 1991.[4] Therefore, increased consumer purchases did not lead to more jobs for either blue-collar workers or for the manufacturing companies as a whole. The 1974–1991 trend continued in 1992–1993. Layoffs in those years at General Motors, IBM, and Boeing, which were typical of many large companies, received much publicity in the news media.

Of course, the loss of factory jobs was not evenly spread. Worst hit were the primary metal industries, such as aluminum and steel, in which employment dropped by more than 40 percent over this twelve-year period. Employment in those factories making fabricated metal products dropped by 21 percent. On the other hand, employment in the plastics industry, whose products in part replaced metals, rose by 5 percent. Employment in the paper and chemical industries held level, whereas the number of employees working in printing and publishing actually rose by 24 percent—perhaps reflecting all that junk mail and the newspapers bloated by advertising.[4]

Nevertheless, overall manufacturing employment moved down, whereas personal consumption expenditures for both durable and nondurable goods went up. What is the

## Employment in Manufacturing

explanation for the missing 7 million workers? Those who have observed the influx of Toyota and Mercedes automobiles, as well as Japanese-made televisions and VCRs might guess at a possible reason for this: the increased consumer expenditures were for <u>imported</u> goods, which of course did not require any American workers to produce. Politicians sometimes refer to the importing of goods as "the exporting of jobs." Maybe these 7 million jobs disappeared to Mexico and other low-wage countries, accompanied by a large sucking sound as they left.

Closer examination, however, shows that increased imports of consumer goods were <u>not</u> the determining factor in the decrease in manufacturing employment. Of course, U.S. exports of consumer products also increased during the 1980s. One must look not at imports alone but at the balance of trade, considering both imports and exports, since exports of consumer goods <u>increase</u> employment of U.S. workers. The following table, which is in constant 1987 dollars, shows what happened to the exports and imports of consumer goods during this period.

## CHAPTER II

### EXPORTS AND IMPORTS OF CONSUMER GOODS IN CONSTANT DOLLARS[5]
(Billions of 1987 dollars)

| | 1979 | 1991 |
|---|---|---|
| **Exports** | | |
| Automotive vehicles, engines and parts | 28.7 | 36.3 |
| Durable consumer goods, excluding automotive | 9.4 | 21.6 |
| Nondurable consumer goods | 7.4 | 19.2 |
| Total consumer goods exports | 45.5 | 77.1 |
| | | |
| **Imports** | | |
| Automotive vehicles, engines and parts | 42.7 | 75.7 |
| Durable consumer goods, excluding automotive | 23.5 | 50.6 |
| Nondurable consumer goods | 17.3 | 44.8 |
| Total consumer goods imports | 83.5 | 171.1 |
| | | |
| **Balance of Trade** | | |
| Durable consumer goods, including automotive | -28.1 | -68.4 |
| Nondurable consumer goods | -9.9 | -25.6 |
| Balance of trade— consumer goods | -38.0 | -94.0 |

Both exports and imports of consumer goods, expressed in constant dollars, increased dramatically between 1979 and 1991 as world trade burgeoned. The unfavorable balance of trade in consumer goods also approximately doubled during this period. In either year, however, this unfavorable trade balance was a small percentage of total expenditures on consumer goods. The $94.0 billion unfavorable balance in 1991 was 6.5 percent of the total expenditures on consumer goods of $1,456 billion (both figures in constant 1987 dollars). The <u>increase</u> in the unfavorable balance between 1979 and 1991 of $56.0 billion represents

## Employment in Manufacturing

only 3.8 percent of the total consumer goods expenditures. (Because trade figures are at wholesale value and the consumer expenditures are at retail value, a corrected figure to allow for retail markup would be about 5 percent.) Thus, the effect of increased imports on employment of production workers was approximately 5 percent of the 15.1 million jobs at the beginning of the period, or about 750,000 jobs lost for this reason. The large sucking sound turns out to have been a small sipping sound.

One reason that increased imports of consumer goods did not have a more significant effect on employment is that relatively few U.S. companies were in businesses seriously affected by imports. The Department of Labor recently analyzed our foreign trade between 1982 and 1987 and concluded that employment in import-sensitive industries was only 11 percent of total manufacturing employment.[6]

If "export of jobs" did not lead to this paradox of more consumption but fewer jobs, what did? Although there were a number of reasons, the main explanation for this phenomenon is that over the same period the productivity of workers increased. Fewer workers were required to produce more goods. According to the Department of Labor, the index of productivity for manufacturing workers went from 94.4 in 1980 to 125.7 in 1990.[7] This increase in productivity is sufficient to account for all of the missing jobs. It might be argued that there is a limit to how far these productivity increases can go and that eventually more consumer demand will, indeed, mean more jobs. The experience with jobs in agriculture, however, which have dropped from 7 million in 1950 to 3 million today, shows the extent to which productivity improvements can eventually reduce employment.

Two interrelated trends seem likely to have been the principal causes of the continued growth in productivity of manufacturing workers and the consequent loss of manufacturing jobs. The first is technological, arising from further development of automation. The substitution of robots for

# CHAPTER II

human labor has proceeded more slowly than originally projected but nevertheless is continuing to eliminate assembly-line jobs. A robot welding machine is not only cheaper to employ than a human laborer but also produces more uniform welds. Of course, automation does not necessarily involve robots; a device as simple as a conveyor can reduce labor in the transport of goods.

The similar technological displacement of human clerks by computers has also come more slowly than originally forecast. Nevertheless, the massive job cuts in the clerical ranks in the early 1990s show that the clerical phase of the industrial revolution has finally arrived.

In his first novel, *Player Piano*, published in 1952, the novelist Kurt Vonnegut foresaw the trend of increasing production of consumer goods accompanied by lower employment. In Vonnegut's future America, those working in the automated factories would be a privileged few. Most of the rest of the populace would be employed either by the Army or by the Reconstruction and Reclamation Corps, known as the Reeks and Wrecks. Those in the Reeks and Wrecks would perform what are essentially make-work public-sector jobs, such as grading and re-grading gravel roads.[8] Admittedly, this is fiction. However, even if we do not reach the bleak end point depicted by Vonnegut, the trend of increasing manufacturing productivity and decreasing manufacturing employment is all too evident.

A further technological factor that in the long run will reduce both the amount of consumer goods produced and the labor to produce them is the technical improvement in the products. Thirty years ago, automobile tires were expected to last for 10,000 miles. The new steel-belted radial tires now last at least for 35,000 miles, reducing tire demand by two-thirds. Automobiles formerly ran for 20 miles or less on a gallon of gasoline. When the present fleet is replaced by automobiles such as those now used in Europe and Japan that go 40 miles on one gallon, only half as many

## Employment in Manufacturing

gallons of gasoline need be produced. Moreover, automobiles themselves are lasting longer before they need be junked. Those who could afford to do so used to trade in a car after five years or 50,000 miles, whichever came first. A more usual mileage figure for trade-in now is 100,000, with many cars now running satisfactorily after 200,000 miles. When, as seems possible, automobiles eventually become as well-built as the Douglas DC-3 airplane, many of which are still carrying passengers fifty years after they were manufactured, the country will require less than 2 million new cars a year as replacements. The above examples are all drawn from the automobile industry, since that is one we all know, but one can see the same phenomenon in other durable goods such as refrigerators as well as in nondurable goods such as long-lasting fluorescent light bulbs. We simply will not need as many of any of these items because they will incorporate technological improvements that will make them last longer.

In most cases, the longer-lasting items cost more and are priced higher than the products they replace. Often, the increase in unit price fully compensates for the drop in the number of units so that the sales of the manufacturer may stay level or even increase. With fewer units to produce, however, the number of production employees goes down.

Responsible in part both for the productivity improvements and for the improvement in quality and durability of the manufactured products is the second trend—a new management philosophy known as Total Quality Management (TQM). Although the concept was originated in the United States by management consultants such as W. Edwards Deming before World War II, it came to fruition in Japan in the 1950s, and since the early 1980s has been widely adopted back in the United States and in Europe. Basically it entails the direct involvement of the factory worker in assuring that the products manufactured are of the highest quality. The system also welcomes suggestions from

## CHAPTER II

the workers on improvements in manufacturing methods to achieve both lower labor costs and higher quality. Those companies adopting TQM compete for the Malcolm Baldrige National Quality Awards. (Another coveted prize is the Shingo Prize for Excellence in American Manufacturing, named for a Japanese consultant.)[9]

Those companies adopting TQM have not, in general, seen the drop in the number of production jobs that their productivity improvements would normally imply. The explanation is that their higher-quality products and prompt delivery schedules give them an advantage over their competitors who have not adopted TQM. Thus, the TQM firms have seen their sales increase enough to compensate for the increased productivity, requiring the same number or more workers. These sales increases, however, have come at the expense of loss of sales (and the layoff of employees) by the non-TQM competitors. The net result is a loss of jobs in the industry as a whole.

In addition to Total Quality Management, many companies are aiming specifically at job elimination through a technique known as "re-engineering." Although re-engineering often involves some of the same techniques as TQM such as work teams and the involvement of lower-level employees in decision making, it emphasizes reorganizing assembly lines and offices to simplify and speed the flow of work. Re-engineering is applicable not only to manufacturing companies but also to service firms. A recent article in *The Wall Street Journal* quotes estimates that this may eliminate as many as 25 million U.S. jobs.[10]

An additional trend that seems likely in the future to affect both production of consumer goods and employment in their manufacture is a revulsion on the part of some of the public at the excesses of consumerism. This first appeared on the national scene in the "Hippy" movement of the 1960's. Partly as a result of wide publicity to the spending habits of Imelda Marcos, Donald and Ivana Trump, and

## Employment in Manufacturing

Leona Helmsley, there is now a sense throughout a growing portion of the middle class that it is wrong for Americans to consume such a disproportionate share of the world's resources. There is a feeling that production of <u>unneeded</u> consumer goods represents a waste—of the materials and energy used in their manufacture and in the extra load on the environment from refuse produced in their manufacture. A popular bumper sticker reads, "We should live simply so that others can simply live." So far, the effect in the United States of this desire to abate consumerism has probably been limited but likely will be more important in the future.

In any case, as the table earlier in the chapter showed, the increase in the demand for consumer goods has not been sufficient to overcome the above trends of technology-driven productivity increases, improved management practices, and disillusionment with consumerism. The Imelda Marcos Factor turns out not to be as powerful a force in influencing employment as Total Quality Management and re-engineering. These trends are likely to continue. In a projection of employment in the United States to the year 2005, the Bureau of Labor Statistics estimates a further loss of 500,000 manufacturing jobs between 1992 and 2005.[11]

Some economists also have recognized that unlimited production of consumer goods is not the answer to our economic and social problems, though such views are still in the minority. In his 1899 book, *The Theory of the Leisure Class*, the American economist Thorstein Veblen invented the phrase "conspicuous consumption" to describe expenditures made not for comfort or use but to impress others.[12] Thirty-five years ago, the economist John Kenneth Galbraith wrote:[13]

> To furnish a barren room is one thing. To crowd in furniture until the foundation buckles is quite another. To have failed to solve the problem of producing

# CHAPTER II

goods would have been to continue man in his oldest and most grievous misfortune. But to fail to see that we have solved it and to proceed thence to the next task, would be fully as tragic.

Because of its relative ineffectiveness in creating jobs, the adverse effects on the environment, and the tendency of humans to accumulate more material goods than they can possibly use, the strategy of generating job growth through increased production of consumer goods probably is the least desirable of the eight means for increasing employment that were listed in the Introduction.

This is not to say that manufacturing is unimportant. For a number of reasons, it is valuable to maintain a strong manufacturing sector. Probably the most important is the production of strategic goods for our national defense. In both the First and Second World Wars, the U.S. manufacturing capacity provided the Allies with the margin for victory, and the world is not yet safe enough to assume that there will not be future wars. Further, in order for there to be effective research and development of new products, it is necessary to have this R & D closely associated with manufacture.

However, just as it is important to have a strong agricultural sector, even though we cannot look to agriculture for job growth, in the future we should not expect even a strong manufacturing sector to be a major source of new jobs. The next chapter will examine the alternative of increasing jobs through encouraging more expenditures in the consumer-services sector.

## Chapter III

## EMPLOYMENT IN SERVICES:

## Physicians, Beauticians, and Auto Technicians

*F*or many readers, the category of "services" conjures up pictures of fast-food restaurants with legions of low-paid hamburger flippers. The service sector, however, is a broad one that includes a large number of highly paid jobs requiring extensive education. These range from doctors and lawyers to consulting hydrogeologists and professors of agricultural economics.

Consumer services in 1991 constituted 37 percent of the total U.S. economy, compared with 30 percent for consumer goods. The service-producing sector is not only larger but also has grown faster than the goods-producing sector. Although between 1979 and 1991, the consumer-goods-producing sector increased by 26 percent, the consumer-service-producing sector grew by 39 percent.[1] In terms of generating jobs, the service sector has done much better than the goods sector. The following table is based on employment classifications used by the Bureau of Labor Statistics and the Bureau of the Census. These agencies group all jobs outside of agriculture, manufacturing, mining, and construction in a broad "service-producing sector," which includes transportation, wholesale and retail trade, finance, and government as well as "service industries." The

## CHAPTER III

latter includes components such as hotels, health care, and auto repair. The following table shows the growth in personal consumption expenditures for services from 1979 to 1991 and the corresponding jobs, both in the overall service-producing sector and in the specific service industries.

### CONSUMER EXPENDITURES FOR SERVICES
(Billions of 1987 Dollars)[1]
AND EMPLOYMENT IN SERVICES (Millions)[2]

| YEAR | PERSONAL CONSUMER SERVICES EXPEND. | TOTAL SERVICE SECTOR EMPLOYMENT | SERVICE INDUSTRIES EMPLOYMENT |
|---|---|---|---|
| 1979 | $1,296 (Billion) | 63.4 (Million) | 17.1 (Million) |
| 1980 | 1,324 | 64.7 | 17.9 |
| 1981 | 1,344 | 65.6 | 18.6 |
| 1982 | 1,369 | 65.8 | 19.0 |
| 1983 | 1,421 | 66.9 | 19.7 |
| 1984 | 1,473 | 69.8 | 20.8 |
| 1985 | 1,537 | 72.7 | 22.0 |
| 1986 | 1,576 | 75.0 | 23.0 |
| 1987 | 1,637 | 77.5 | 24.2 |
| 1988 | 1,698 | 80.4 | 25.7 |
| 1989 | 1,732 | 83.0 | 27.1 |
| 1990 | 1,773 | 85.0 | 28.2 |
| 1991 | 1,803 | 85.2 | 28.8 |

Ratio 91/79         1.39              1.34              1.68

Not only did consumer expenditures on services rise regularly during this period but employment rose _every_ year,

## Employment in Services

both in the broad service-producing sector (which includes transportation, wholesale and retail trade, and financial services) and the specific service industries. This is in sharp contrast to the consumer goods sector, where employment fell even as personal consumption expenditures for goods rose. Further, the total number of jobs involved in the service-producing sector (85 million) is approximately <u>four times</u> the total number of jobs in the whole goods-producing sector (23 million). The latter figure includes mining and construction as well as manufacturing and counts overhead employees as well as blue-collar workers. There is no question that the service-producing sector has been the engine of job growth.

The predominance of the service sector in the total economy is also the explanation for the much-quoted figure that most new jobs in the last decade have come from small businesses with fewer than twenty employees. Unlike the manufacturing sector, in which the manufacturing technologies and economies of scale favor large firms like General Motors and Texaco, most small service firms can survive along with larger firms. The mom-and-pop delicatessen coexists with the supermarket, and the local bar and grill serves a different clientele from McDonald's fast-food outlet. In the profession of law, small firms are the rule, with the large Wall Street firms the exception. The growing trend of franchising a successful idea for a service business such as one-hour film developing also favors small firms. Since most of the growth of jobs has been in the service sector and most of the firms in the service sector are small, it follows that most of the job growth occurs in small firms.

Although the output of the service sector will continue to grow, this sector in the future may no longer be as strong an engine for job growth. The management technique of re-engineering mentioned in the previous chapter is increasingly being applied in service-sector firms to increase productivity and thus reduce employment. A recent *Wall*

# CHAPTER III

*Street Journal* article reported that through re-engineering a financial services company in Louisville, Kentucky, reduced its number of employees on its payroll from 1,900 people to 1,100, while its business rose 25 percent. A consultant quoted in the same article predicted a loss of 600,000 to 700,000 jobs through re-engineering in the banking industry alone in the period from 1993 to 2000.[3]

The service-producing sector, as defined by the U.S. Department of Commerce, encompasses a wide variety of businesses. These include transportation, communication, wholesale distribution and retail stores, insurance and real estate, and government at all levels, as well as consumer services. In this book, transportation and communications employment will be covered separately in Chapter V on Infrastructure and government employment in Chapter VI; this chapter will concentrate on services per se.

As might be expected from its importance in the economy, the service industry with the largest number of employees is health care. Between 1980 and 1990, the health services industry added 2.9 million jobs, an average growth of 4.1 percent. Hospitals alone added 1,300,000 jobs, and personal care and nursing facilities an additional 520,000. This growth rate was 1.5 times the growth rate in the rest of the service-producing sector, excluding health services. Because of the indispensable nature of its services, the health-care sector is little affected by the ups and down of the economy.[4] This sector employed more than 8.5 million people in 1992 and is projected to grow to 12.5 million in the year 2005.[5] Included in these totals are highly paid physicians and low-paid hospital cleaners. Of course, these projections were made before the Clinton proposals for changes in the health-care structure, and it is unclear how these proposals, or alternatives enacted by Congress, will affect employment. Since the thrust of all of the plans, however, is toward universal coverage and because the

## Employment in Services

aging population will require more health-care services, the above projections seem reasonable.

In terms of number of employees, the next two service categories are financial (which includes banks, brokers, insurance, and real estate) and eating and drinking places. In 1992, employees in finance numbered 6.6 million, and those working for restaurants and bars also numbered 6.6 million. Of course, the financial people include some of the highest-paid individuals in the nation, whereas the restaurant and bar group include some of the lowest. On the other hand, $15,000 clerks are included among the financial people, and $100,000 chefs are listed along with the hamburger flippers. The Department of Commerce projects that the financial ranks will swell by 1.4 million employees by the year 2005, and the food and drink crews will grow by 2.2 million.[5]

Included in the service category are business services such as advertising, personnel recruiting, data processing, and guard and security services. These businesses totaled 5.3 million people in 1992, and are forecast to grow to 8.4 million in 2005.[5] As in the above categories, the business-service group includes both low-paying jobs such as security guards and highly paid positions such as advertising account directors.

Another 1.2 million people work in businesses classified by the Department of Commerce as "Amusement and Recreation Services."[5] These businesses provide entertainment and thus, presumably, happiness for the populace. This seems a particularly promising area for growth in employment. In our age, the classification of "Amusement and Recreation Services" corresponds to the "circuses" in the Roman poet and satirist Juvenal's statement, "Two things only the people anxiously desire—bread and circuses."[6]

As pointed out in previous chapters, the economic problem of supplying basic human needs— "bread" —has

## CHAPTER III

long been solved in this country. We use only 3 percent of our labor force to grow not only the wheat for our bread but also the greatest variety of other foodstuffs that the world has ever known. And we still have ample wheat left over for export to other countries.

As for "circuses," we have a number of different forms. Most prominent is television. A small proportion of television programming is meant to be educational, but the overwhelming share is aimed at amusement of the viewers. Even the morning news programs of the major networks now consist of five minutes of news and twenty-five minutes of human-interest stories, sports news, and commercials, a combination known as "Infotainment." Closely allied to television are the motion picture industry and the industries that supply video games such as Nintendo as well as videos of movies for home consumption.

A somewhat different kind of circus is supplied by amateur and professional sports. Many of these, such as the major professional baseball, football, hockey, and basketball leagues, depend on television for a large share of their revenues. Amateur sports, too, have assumed a circus character, with displays ranging from the Rose Bowl to the Olympics, the latter of which until recently professed to be the province of amateur athletics. A different, but still circuslike, spectacle is provided by the various forms of racing—horse, dog, and automotive.

The interest in sports is enhanced by gambling on the outcomes of the games and races. Moreover, pure gambling is also a major form of entertainment. A substantial portion of the populace either places bets on the state lottery at its local newsstand, plays Bingo at the local church, or visits the casinos on riverboats or Indian reservations, among other locations.

The performing arts also provide a circus for the populace. The circus atmosphere is most noticeable at performances of popular music stars from country-and-

## Employment in Services

western to rock and hip-hop, but it is also a component of the amusements of the upper class, such as the Metropolitan Opera and the American Ballet Theatre.

The value that society places on sports and entertainment figures is shown by their income. Topping the list is singer Michael Jackson, who signed a contract with SONY in 1991 that could return him $1 billion (although his highly publicized personal problems may prevent him from reaching that figure.) Boxer Evander Holyfield earned $60.5 million in 1991, about double boxer Mike Tyson's $30 million. Talk show hostess Oprah Winfrey received $40 million. Cult figure Madonna earned $30 million in 1991 and probably more in 1992 when her book on sex was published. Movie star Sylvester Stallone was paid $20 million for *Rocky V.* Baseball player Bobby Bonilla received $6.1 million from the New York Mets, and hockey player Ruben Serra of the New York Rangers was paid $5 million. For comparison, the chief executive officers of the 25 largest U.S. corporations averaged $3 million in compensation in 1991.[7]

Amusement is also provided by travel. It can be pure entertainment, such as that found on a cruise ship, or have some educational content, as is purported to be provided by Colonial Williamsburg and Disney World. (The writer Umberto Eco has labeled the latter experiences as "hyper-reality.")[8] In some of our states, tourism now ranks as one of the major industries; it tops the list in Hawaii.

But perhaps the most important amusement in America today is shopping. Retail stores in 1992 employed almost 13 million people, a figure projected to grow by 2.3 million by the year 2005.[9] Many Americans shop not because they really need the items they are purchasing but for the pure joy of shopping. A popular T-shirt identifies the wearer as "Born To SHOP." The success of shopping malls is founded on this premise. Some of the most recent malls, such as the Mall of the Americas outside of Minneapolis, Minnesota, expressly combine an amusement park with a

# CHAPTER III

vast assortment of specialty retail shops and fast-food outlets. Although the stores and restaurants in the malls are classified as part of the service sector, they obviously depend on the goods-producing sector for the items they sell.

One way to increase the demand for consumer services in the recreation/entertainment sector would be to give workers more leisure to use these services. Chapters IX and X will explore mechanisms to provide this added leisure through shorter hours of work per week and/or fewer years of work per lifetime. Either strategy would not only provide more leisure to use consumer services such as sports, travel, and entertainment but also would create more jobs by spreading the available work.

Of course, there are a variety of other service-producing industries in addition to health care, retail stores, and those businesses devoted to amusement and entertainment. These include brokerage firms and law offices, as well as barber shops and pizza parlors. Also included are all of the repair industries, including automotive, watch, and shoe repair.

Those consumer sectors identified earlier in this chapter (health care, food service, amusements, and retail stores) are forecast to require about 11.8 million more employees by the year 2005. Other service areas such as finance, legal, and accounting, which serve both consumers and business, are calculated to require about 2 million additional people. The entire service sector, excluding government, transportation, and communications, which are covered separately in later chapters, is forecast by the Bureau of Labor Statistics to provide 20 million more jobs between 1992 and 2005.[10]

Consumer services have an advantage over consumer goods in that it is much more difficult and often impossible to substitute an imported service for the locally available service. One can easily buy a Honda instead of a Chevrolet,

## Employment in Services

but it is much more difficult to employ a Japanese real estate agent to sell your house in Scarsdale than to use the local Century 21 branch. It is also much more convenient to use a local doctor or lawyer than to consult with a British physician or solicitor. As a result, both exports and imports of services are only about 20 percent of the value of exports and imports of goods, and the United States has consistently run a favorable balance of payments in services. Thus, a job in the service area is much less likely to be displaced by imports than a manufacturing job.

Although the next four chapters will review other sources of job creation, such as state and local governments, transportation, communication, and construction, the reader will find that none of these will come close to the service-producing sector as a source for new jobs. Because, according to the estimates of the Bureau of Labor Statistics, employment in agriculture will stay constant at 3.3 million workers and employment in manufacturing will shrink by 500,000 workers between 1992 and the year 2005,[11] it is to the service sector that the nation *must* look for employment growth.

Many economists seem unhappy about this trend. This may be in part because the focus of economics has traditionally been upon goods—how to maximize their production and establish their prices. The output of the service sector is much more difficult to measure, and any measure of productivity is more difficult to establish. (Is a high-paid baseball player more "productive" than a rookie because he is paid more?)

Also it is true that many service-producing jobs, such as those of auditors and employee benefits consultants, have manufacturing firms as important customers. Most of these business services, however, also have other firms in the service sector for clients. The auditors audit the books of the benefits consultants, and the benefits consultants

# CHAPTER III

help the auditors design their executive compensation packages. Because of the growth of the whole service sector, it is the service businesses that will provide the growing market for business services. As mentioned in the last chapter, there are a number of reasons why it is important that the United States have a strong manufacturing sector as well as a strong agricultural sector, but in neither case do these sectors provide growth in employment or growth in demand for business services.

Probably there is less reason to mourn the passing of the manufacturing sector as a major source of employment in the twenty-first century than there was to mourn the passing of the family farm in the first half of the twentieth century. At least, the family farm provided an independent existence close to nature, with work following the natural rhythms of the days and seasons. Manufacturing work, on the other hand, since the inception of the Industrial Revolution has been dull, repetitive, and far removed from the sun and the soil. The English Luddites, who attempted to smash textile machinery in the early 1800's because the automated looms and spinning jennies replaced satisfying craft work with monotonous drudgery in dismal surroundings, had a valid point. Although factory conditions have improved, the jobs on the punch presses or assembly lines of manufacturing plants must still be some of the least satisfying in the work force. Even the short-order cook at the local diner has more variety in his or her work than the operator of a plastic molding machine.

Over the period since the Second World War, Americans have shown that they want ever more consumer services, and their appetite shows no signs of diminishing. After discussing the other possible sources of job growth, we shall return in Chapter VIII to the service sector and suggest ways to encourage the trend of service-industry growth.

## Chapter IV

## EMPLOYMENT FROM TECHNOLOGY:

### From the Space Station to Virtual Reality

*M*ost of the nation's present manufacturing jobs stem from inventions made in the past century. The automobile, aircraft, and electronics industries did not exist one hundred years ago. Although individual inventors such as the Wright Brothers, Thomas Edison, and Henry Ford played a large role in the past, the source of new products and jobs seems increasingly to be large laboratories. One of the ways that the government can have an influence on employment in the future is by encouraging those research projects in its own laboratories and in industrial establishments that have the potential for providing future employment for a significant number of workers.

Since the Second World War, the United States has spent large sums on military research and development. Approximately two-thirds of the federal funding for research and development in the 1980s was in the national defense area.[1] This research resulted in our long-range nuclear missiles, the Stealth Bomber, and nuclear-powered submarines, all of which opened up new jobs. With the end of the Cold War, military research and development is no longer a viable way to stimulate employment. Those employed in the government laboratories devoted to military research and

## CHAPTER IV

development, however, are naturally unwilling to stop doing what they know how to do—develop weapons. Further, even in the nonmilitary area, the government tradition has been to spend money on research for "big science." There has developed a science-industrial complex analogous to the military-industrial complex.

As a result of pressures from the science-industrial complex, two major research projects were commenced—the space station *Freedom* sponsored by the National Aeronautics and Space Administration (NASA) and the Super-Conducting Super-Collider constructed in Texas by the Department of Energy. Both projects have been controversial.

When the space station was first proposed in 1984, NASA estimated that it would cost $8 billion to procure the parts, transport them to space, and assemble the station. By 1993, the official estimate had risen to $30 billion, and the U.S Comptroller General estimated the real cost at $118 billion, not including operating costs during the life of the station. The justifications for the station include the ability to do research in a zero-gravity environment and the need to study the effects of long stays in space on humans as preparation for an eventual trip to Mars. Nevertheless, reviews by both the President's Office of Science and Technology Policy and the Space Science Board of the National Research Council concluded that the station as currently designed did not meet the basic research requirements for either microgravity materials research or life sciences research. The project survived because procurement of the station's components was spread over a number of congressional districts. NASA claimed that the project would mean 100,000 jobs.[2] Once the construction phase was over, however, those permanently employed would be the four astronauts living in the station and their supporting staff, which would probably be around 10,000. This is not

## Employment From Technology

an effective way to solve the long-term unemployment problem.

The Super-Conducting Super Collider (SSC) was a somewhat smaller project, with a cost estimated in 1992 to total $8.25 billion. (Shortly before it was canceled by Congress, the estimated cost had risen to nearly $12 billion.) It was a fifty-mile electronic racetrack constructed in Waxahachie, Texas, to accelerate protons to a velocity closer to the speed of light than ever before produced. At the time the protons collide, they would possess twenty times more energy than particles produced by existing accelerators. The hope was that the collisions would produce new particles to test current theories. such as "superstring" and "technicolor," proposed to explain and unify the fundamental forces.[3] This is research at its purest, with no expectation of any practical application. After the initial construction, the laboratory was expected to employ about 2,000 people, at a capital cost of $6 million per person employed.[4] Thus, it would have had even less impact on employment than the space station. Partly because of large cost overruns and partly because of a disenchantment with scientific megaprojects by Congress, the partially completed project was canceled in October 1993.

In sharp contrast to these megaprojects is the field of photovoltaics, the technical term for solar cells that turn sunlight into electricity. This effort does receive some government support; the Department of Energy budgeted $63.5 million for solar-cell research in fiscal 1993. However, most of the research is being privately financed by a number of different firms outside of the science-industrial complex. So far, most of the market is for small devices such as watches and calculators. In 1992, however, a major test began in Davis, California of a program called PVUSA— Photovoltaics for Utility Scale Applications. This facility will test 20-kilowatt systems for reliability and cost. Several manufacturers, such as Energy Conversion Devices in

## CHAPTER IV

Detroit, Michigan, and Entech in Dallas, Texas, believe that their current technology would be competitive with conventional fuels in a 100-megawatt plant. An alternative approach would be to decentralize power production by putting solar cells on the roofs of residences. Other proposed uses for solar cells include powering fans to ventilate a car sitting in a parking lot and recharging batteries in an electric car that the commuter has left at the railroad station.[5]

The employment effect of a solar cell industry will depend on whether the predominant use of the devices is in central power stations, where the employment effects would be low, or in decentralized rooftop arrays on homes, which might lead to hundreds of thousands of jobs in distribution and service. In either case, the environmental effect of using solar energy rather than fossil fuels to supply our energy needs would be markedly favorable, since solar energy production is not accompanied by either the devastation resulting from coal mining or by the air pollution caused by burning either coal or petroleum-based fuels.

Another area of research and development with a bright future is known as virtual reality, often abbreviated to VR. Although VR depends on sophisticated computers, it differs markedly from the usual computer graphics in two ways: it provides the participant with sound and/or touch simulation as well as visual display, and it is interactive. In one advanced form, the participant wears a helmet that projects three-dimensional pictures on the lenses of the helmet, and the user can manipulate the images with a sensor-equipped glove. The head-mounted stereo screen displays are known as "eyephones" and the gloves as "datagloves." Less-sophisticated systems manipulate the images with a joystick or computer mouse.

The government already recognizes the potential of VR. According to *Business Week*, the U.S. military plans to spend more than $500 million over the next four years on simulations of operations of tanks, airplanes, and other equipment. In this application, VR is a wonderful training tool. The trainee can be challenged with dangerous situations and taught how to cope with them without, in fact, being in physical danger. In 1991, Senator Albert Gore, now Vice President, chaired hearings on the value of VR to American competitiveness, which concluded that we are underinvesting in this technology.[6]

Although VR will involve durable-goods manufacture in the form of computers and displays, eventually it will require much more in the way of computer programming and other services to provide the software for the systems. VR can be used in training operators for power plants and chemical plants at lower cost than the mock-ups of control rooms now used in training. Many of VR's uses will be in the fields of medicine, architecture, and engineering. A California company is using VR to analyze repetitive-stress injuries such as the carpal tunnel syndrome. Engineers are using VR to test the fit of imaginary parts.

Moreover, VR also has vast potential for consumer entertainment. A game center in Chicago that allows players to fight battles from a simulated fighter-plane cockpit sold more than $2 million worth of tickets in its first three months of operation. But the entertainment value of VR need not be confined to arcades. In the future, it could be possible to sit in your armchair and "stroll" around the Taj Mahal in the moonlight, stopping wherever you wished. By so doing, you would be supporting a new industry that could employ many more people than the travel agents it displaced!

It has even been proposed that VR could let the armchair traveler "walk" on the moon or on Mars—without constructing a manned space station. This would be accomplished by using un-manned space probes to photograph the surfaces of the moon and selected planets and transmit the images back to earth. These images could then be manipulated by computer to produce a simulation of a space stroll to be enjoyed by those possessing the proper VR equipment

## CHAPTER IV

and software.[7] The NASA Ames Research Center at Moffett Field, California, is using VR to help plan missions to the moon. According to physicist Shawn Carlson, it will soon be possible to "blend the thrill of human exploration with the safety and cost-effectiveness of robot surrogates."[8]

This is the sort of innovation that the government should support if it wishes to use research to increase employment. In 1993 about 59 percent of the $57 billion federal expenditure on research and development was still spent in the defense area. Another 33 percent went to health, space, and energy, leaving 8 percent for everything else. In a recent article, Don E. Kash of George Mason University and Robert W. Rycroft of George Washington University suggest shifting substantial federal funds away from basic research toward applied R & D for commercial applications. They propose a federally funded but politically insulated corporation that would draw on expertise in government, industry, and academia.[9] The corporation would create networks to spur innovations, both in products and processes, that are likely to lead to commercial success.

Another approach is to have the national weapons laboratories give priority to projects that have commercial as well as military potential. In the past, the Advanced Research Projects Agency (ARPA) has been a leader in computing technologies such as networking and parallel processing that have dual applications. Some of the weapons laboratories are also working directly with industry. In late 1993, the Los Alamos National Laboratory, the birthplace of the atomic bomb, announced it was working with a Minnesota company on new ways of fabricating circuit boards. The Lawrence Livermore National Laboratory has cooperated with a Colorado concern on using advanced X-ray techniques originally developed for nuclear weapons in machines for mammography examinations.[10]

## Employment From Technology

It is in the nature of new technology that the employment effect is long term rather than short term. Thus the effect of new developments probably will not be fully felt by the turn of the century, but 500 thousand additional jobs might result by the year 2005.

## Chapter V

# EMPLOYMENT FROM STRUCTURE AND INFRASTRUCTURE:

## Low-Cost Housing and Maglev Trains

Between 1986 and 1991, employment in the construction industry in the United States remained reasonably steady, ranging between 4.8 million and 5.2 million workers.[1] Of the 5 million workers in 1987, 1.3 million were working for general contractors, 0.8 million (800 thousand) were employed by heavy-construction contractors, and 2.9 million were in special construction trades such as plumbing and heating. Those general contractors specializing in single-family homes and other residential construction employed about 500,000 people directly, with probably an equal number of craftsmen.[2] There is no question that more housing is needed in this country and that building it will increase employment.

Although more commercial buildings will be required in the future, it seems likely that the _rate_ of commercial construction will stay constant or even decrease, so no additional employment can be expected in this sector. On the other hand, construction spending on the infrastructure such as highways, railroads, and airports, and the corresponding employment in this construction, is likely to

## Employment from Structure and Infrastructure

increase. This increase will be most marked in those sectors affected by new technologies, such as public transportation and electronic information distribution. Thus, this chapter will assume that commercial construction is not a likely field for additional jobs and will concentrate on increasing employment in residential construction and in the infrastructure.

The need for more housing in the United States is most visibly illustrated by the homeless, who number at least 250,000. Still, they represent only a small part of the nation's housing shortage. It is estimated that 7.6 million of the nation's housing units are substandard through lack of indoor plumbing or from defective heating, electrical, or sewerage systems. Another 2.2 million households live in overcrowded conditions. In housing, particularly low-cost housing, the problem is not lack of need or demand but rather how to finance the construction. Between 1975 and 1983 a federal program known as Section 8 was responsible for the construction of 850,000 new housing units, but this program was eliminated by the Reagan administration.[3] If a way could be found to finance a new program for low-cost housing, the employment effects would be significant. As noted above, about 500,000 people are now employed by contractors specializing in residential construction, with probably an equal number of craftsmen also involved. In 1992 there were 1.1 million new housing starts.[4] If this could be increased by 550,000 units each year, which would eliminate the low-cost housing shortage in about fifteen years, between 500,000 and 600,000 new jobs would be created. It appears, however, that the private sector will not build these houses without substantial government incentives. A new program equivalent to the old Section 8 is needed.

In this chapter, we are considering not only structures such as housing but also the infrastructure. One of the most promising infrastructure developments is the construction of

## CHAPTER V

what is known as "information highways." Rather than concrete, these "highways" are constructed of fiber-optic cables. The cables will be combined with satellites, computerized switches, and millions of lines of software code to provide a communications network for voice, video, and data linking all the homes and offices in America—and eventually most of the world. The forecasting firm DRI/McGraw-Hill estimates that the U.S. telecommunications industry will spend $325 billion between 1994 and 2004 to build these highways.[5]

Unlike the concrete highways financed by the state and federal governments, it appears that most of the enormous cost of these information highways will be privately financed. In a pilot project, the New Jersey Bell subsidiary of Bell Atlantic is planning to spend $1.5 billion in the state of New Jersey by the year 2010 on a network that will combine fiber-optic cables with conventional copper transmission lines.[6]

When the national network is completed, it will have the capability of providing up to one thousand separate communications channels to each recipient. This opens up the possibility of two-way communication for shopping so that a viewer could receive the equivalent of a catalog, select, and order an item through interactive television. Other possible uses are two-way links between physicians and their patients and between teachers and distant classrooms. *Time* magazine recently forecast, "People will be able to call up on their screen virtually anything the culture produces, from the latest Hollywood movie to lessons in chess, from an old episode of *The Twilight Zone* to this morning's newspaper, custom-edited for individual readers."[7] The employment impact of this development is unclear but, based on average productivity, expenditures nationwide at the rate of $30 billion per year, as forecast by DRI/McGraw Hill, should translate into at least 1.5 million jobs. Further,

## Employment from Structure and Infrastructure

these expenditures and the resulting jobs will all be in the private sector.

Another infrastructure development that has excited wide interest is high-speed intercity trains. The United States is far behind both Japan and Europe in this development. Japan completed its first line for the Bullet Train in 1964, and train service has now captured at least 80 percent of the market between Tokyo and Osaka, 320 miles away. The line operates at a profit and paid off its World Bank construction loan in the 1970s. Since opening, this and other Japanese high-speed train lines have carried more than 3 billion passengers at speeds up to 170 miles per hour without a single passenger fatality or injury. In Europe, France's TGV trains also have a perfect safety record. The Atlantic line in France uses 95 trains, which operate at speeds up to 185 miles per hour. It was built with government subsidies, but the newer Southeast line was built from internally generated funds and from borrowing on the private capital markets. Germany too has built new trackage and upgraded existing lines for its ICE trains, which are as fast as the French TGVs. Italy has started construction of its high-speed rail network, estimated to cost $15 billion.[8]

One of the factors driving the move to high-speed trains in Europe and Japan is their superiority to airplanes and automobiles in energy efficiency and its consequently favorable effect on the environment. The following table prepared by the French transport ministry shows fuel consumption per passenger-kilometer for various vehicles.

## CHAPTER V

### FUEL CONSUMPTION OF TRAINS, CARS, AND PLANES

| VEHICLE TYPE | Fuel Used By Vehicle 100% Load | Average Load Factor (% Capacity) | Fuel Used Average Load |
|---|---|---|---|
| HIGH-SPEED TRAIN | 11 | 65% | 17 |
| SMALL CAR - HIGHWAY | 20 | 57% | 35 |
| LARGE CAR - HIGHWAY | 20 | 40% | 50 |
| AIRLINER | 35 | 68% | 52 |

Thus, a high-speed train traveling at 160 miles per hour (260 kilometers per hour) uses only about one-third the fuel to carry a passenger a unit distance as does an airplane or large automobile and approximately one-half the fuel consumed by a small automobile traveling the same distance. The advantage to the ecology of using trains rather than airplanes or automobiles is self-evident.[8]

Unlike Europe and Japan, the United States has been slow to move to a high-speed rail system. Neither the private sector nor the government-subsidized Amtrak has had the cash flow required to build the new roadbeds that are required for high-speed trains equivalent to the French TGV and the Japanese Bullet Train. The Reagan administration sharply reduced the subsidy to Amtrak, and the Clinton administration has given higher priority to repair of highways and bridges than to new mass transportation such as high-speed trains.

In the United States, the first high-speed rail line will use a new technology known as "maglev," which stands for magnetic levitation. In this system, the electric power that propels the train also provides the energy to levitate the train above the track to provide smooth and nearly frictionless

## Employment from Structure and Infrastructure

motion. Although maglev is not as energy efficient as steel-wheel transport, the technical trick of magnetic levitation seems likely to be the decisive factor in persuading Americans to move from their automobiles to a train. The first U.S. maglev high-speed trains, to be built by a German consortium called Transrapid International, will cover 13.3 miles between Orlando International Airport and that city's Grand Central Station at a speed up to 250 miles per hour. Estimated to cost $596 million, the project is privately financed.[9]

Other proposals for high-speed, steel-wheel or maglev lines include Las Vegas to Los Angeles and Miami to Tampa. The Las Vegas–Los Angeles route has been analyzed in most detail and is estimated to cost $2.5 billion for the 230 miles of maglev guideway and forty vehicles. It probably would be privately financed.[10] Another route under study for high-speed trains, probably maglev, is from New York City to Albany along the New York Thruway and from Albany continuing to Boston along the Thruway extension and the Massachusetts Turnpike. Estimated costs are in the range of $20 million per mile. It is believed fares would be less than current air fares and the time from city center to city center would be less than with the current air shuttle.[11] Development of these high-speed intercity links would be greatly facilitated by the passage of a bill, already introduced by Senator Patrick Moynihan of New York, that would make possible the use of the median strip of the interstate highway system for high-speed trains.

Since the projects are so tentative at this point, it is impossible to forecast the employment effect. However, it probably will be substantially less than the employment for the fiber-optic cable project, perhaps on the order of 100,000.

## Chapter VI

# EMPLOYMENT IN GOVERNMENT:

## Teachers and Bureaucrats

*I*n 1937 approximately 10 million Americans were working in agriculture, whereas only 3 million were employed in state and local government, plus another 800,000 who were working for the federal government.[1] Since then, and especially during the last twenty years, employment in the government has been one of the great growth sectors in the economy. By 1990, the employment figures in agriculture and government were reversed—3 million farm workers and more than 10 million government employees at the local level alone. We have made wonderful strides in improving productivity on the farms, thus freeing up 7 million farmers to become government bureaucrats. The following table shows the increases at the federal, state, and local governmental levels during the recent twenty-year period.

Employment in Government

Government Employment ('000 omitted)[2]

| Year | Federal | State | Local | Total |
|---|---|---|---|---|
| 1970 | 2,731 | 2,664 | 7,158 | 12,553 |
| 1980 | 2,866 | 3,610 | 9,765 | 16,241 |
| 1990 | 3,085 | 4,303 | 10,934 | 18,322 |
| 1990/1970 | 1.13 | 1.62 | 1.53 | 1.46 |

Thus, although federal employment went up by 13 percent over this twenty-year period, state and local employees increased by 62 and 53 percent, respectively. The principal functions at the state and local levels are education, health, highways, police and fire protection, and public welfare. The 1991 employment in these functions was as follows ('000 omitted).[3]

|  | State | Local |
|---|---|---|
| Education | 1,999 | 6,074 |
| Health | 724 | 790 |
| Highways | 259 | 305 |
| Protection | 87 | 1,015 |
| Welfare | 217 | 275 |

In education, most of the state employees work at the state universities, and most of the local government employees are involved in elementary and secondary education. There is little doubt that more teachers are needed at all levels. In the first place, because the children of the baby boomers are now moving through the school system, there is a larger population to educate. Beyond that, as will be further discussed in Chapter XII, international comparisons show that American children are not being educated as well as their European and Asian counterparts, particularly in mathematics and science. Most educators agree that the

## CHAPTER VI

first step in improving overall performance is to ensure adequate preschool education through programs such as Head Start. At the elementary level, one way to improve classroom performance is to reduce class size so that the children can receive more individual attention. The number of additional teachers required is directly proportional to this reduction; 20 percent does not seem unreasonable. At the secondary level, a longer school day and more days per year are advocated by those who have looked at how our competitors on the international scene are educating their teenagers. This too will require more teachers. Our state colleges and universities probably need fewer additional people to handle educational needs, but a whole new set of instructors will be required if we implement an apprenticeship program for those students who elect not to go to college. All told, an additional 1 million teachers and administrators probably will be required over the next ten years in government supported schools alone, with perhaps 200,000 additional people needed for additional staff in private schools and colleges.

The 1.4 million government workers in the health field also will increase as the new health plans cover those now left out of the system. 200,000 additional employees each in state and local health services appears to be a minimum increase over the next ten years. Continued efforts to reduce the rate of increase of health-care costs will limit employment increases in the health-care area, but the aging population alone probably will force the hiring of at least the numbers indicated above. (These government employees in the health-service area are in addition to the private-sector health-service employees tabulated in Chapter III on services.)

The remaining areas of employment by state and local governments are highways, police and fire protection, and public welfare. In all three areas, employment growth in the ten years from 1980 to 1990 was slow but steady, totaling

## Employment in Government

about 220,000. A bill recently enacted by Congress will increase federal aid to police departments with the aim of adding 100,000 more policemen and policewomen to local forces. Increased numbers of prisons to house those criminals apprehended by the expanded police forces will also require more guards and prison administrators. Over the next ten years, a further growth of 200,000 employees in these three areas seems reasonable.

In contrast to state and local governments, the size of the federal government is not likely to increase in the near future and may even decrease. The projection of the Bureau of Labor Statistics is that federal employment will decrease by about 150,000 workers between the years 1992 and 2005,[4] Although budget pressures will limit growth of federal employment, past trends of increasing size will be difficult to reverse. For purposes of this book, we shall assume that federal employment stays constant.

The above increases in employment in state and local governments total 1.6 million. This is only about half the increase forecast by the BLS but, again, I believe that the bureau may have underestimated the resistance to additional taxes to support additional services.

## Chapter VII

## EMPLOYMENT FROM CREATIVITY:

### The Arts

*I*n primitive societies, there was no distinction between the artist and the artisan. In fashioning his work, the artisan exercised aesthetic judgment, but his primary interest was in the object created. Nevertheless, almost every society studied by anthropologists seems to have created drawings, pottery, or oral legends that were enjoyed beyond the usefulness of the thing done. The anthropologist Robert Redfield says, "The relation of artist to society includes, therefore, the expression he gives to the more ultimate values and standards of that society. With the priest and the thinker, the artist makes known the collective character of a people, and so unites and directs it by stating its nature and ideals."[1]

By the time of the Classic Period in Greece, the artist was no longer just a master craftsman but an honored creator of aesthetically satisfying art and literature. In the Olympic Games, held every fourth year from June until December, the contests included not only foot racing and wrestling but also artistic and literary competitions. The winners of these intellectual contests too were crowned

## Employment from Creativity

with laurel wreaths. They, along with the warriors and victorious athletes, were national heros.

Our artists and writers are no longer national heros, although some achieve celebrity status, which may be the contemporary equivalent of heroic honor. The majority of those who make their living through writing or through the visual and performing arts work for organizations. Thus, the poets who teach in universities and the graphic artists who create images for Disney have already been included in previous sections devoted to employment in education and entertainment, respectively.

According to the Department of Labor, writers and editors held about 232,000 jobs in the United States in 1990.[2] About 40 percent of them worked for newspapers, magazines, and book publishers. Most of the rest were employed by advertising agencies, worked in radio and television broadcasting, or on journals and newsletters published by business and nonprofit organizations such as professional associations, labor unions, and religious groups. The number of freelance creative writers who support themselves solely through their writing is probably small. Most are likely included in the recent series of reference volumes titled *Contemporary Poets, Contemporary Novelists,* and *Contemporary Dramatists.*[3] These volumes encompassed 800 poets, 600 novelists, and 300 dramatists. Since they include non-Americans writing in English, the American total is probably smaller. Certainly there are relatively few self-supporting poets. Even the current U.S Poet Laureate, Rita Dove, teaches at the University of Virginia. The number of self-supporting novelists who do not also teach is undoubtedly greater than the ranks of poets, but even so the number of authors such as Judith Krantz and Stephen King is limited. Visual artists held about 230,000 jobs in 1990.[2] These included teachers of art, graphic designers, illustrators, fashion artists, cartoonists, animators, and art directors as well as the creators of fine art, such as paintings and

53

## CHAPTER VII

sculpture. Although nearly 60 percent of visual artists are self-employed, most of these work as freelance designers and illustrators rather than as fine artists. Self-supporting fine artists may number from 10,000 to 20,000.

A field closely allied to visual arts is photography. Photographers and camera operators held 120,000 jobs in 1990.[2] About half are self-employed, operating portrait studios or contracting for projects with advertising agencies or magazines. An example of the latter is the hero of the popular novel, *The Bridges of Madison County.*

In the performing arts, musicians and dancers have already been included in the figures for employment in the entertainment industry in Chapter III. The composers of the music played by the musicians and the choreographers of the dance works, however, are a separate category. Since there are only about 8,600 professional dancing jobs,[2] the number of choreographers must be less than 1,000. There are more composers than choreographers, but a great many of them are either teachers in universities or are employed by large organizations such as motion picture or television studios.

Thus, self-employed creative artists in all fields in the United States probably number under 100,000. The increase in leisure time likely in the future will increase the demand for their work. Still, even an optimistic projection of the increased literary and artistic appetites of the American people would probably not result in more than doubling these figures by the year 2005. This would mean an additional 100,000 jobs.

Even to create these jobs probably requires government help. Expanding the funding by the National Endowment for the Arts would help. Another approach that increases the demand for paintings and sculpture, and thus jobs for these artists, is "percent for art" legislation. This kind of legislation, which can be passed at the federal, state, or local level, specifies that a portion of the budget for

## Employment from Creativity

government-sponsored buildings must be set aside for art. Phoenix, Arizona, for instance has such legislation, which has been used to finance 68 projects ranging from sculptures of pots along a main highway to design elements in the Phoenix Solid Waste Management Center.[4]

To increase further the demand for and appreciation of creative art in the United States, we might borrow from the ancient Greeks and have Olympiads of poetry, painting, and drama. There are 3,141 counties in the United States. If each one appointed and supported a poet laureate. an artist laureate, and a composer laureate, this would create about 10,000 more jobs. Then, there could be competition between counties in each state for the state honor, followed by a quadrennial national play-off. At the very least, such an effort would reward and encourage creativity.

# Chapter VIII

# RECAPITULATION:

## The Shortage of Jobs

*I*n the introductory chapter, we estimated that the nation needed to create 40 million new jobs between 1992 and the year 2005—16 million to meet our target of an unemployment rate of only 3 percent, including all those who want full-time jobs, and 24 million to accommodate the growth of the work force by the year 2005.

Where will these jobs come from? Let us summarize our findings from the previous chapters.

| Chapter | Action | Probable employment effect |
|---|---|---|
| II | Increase goods production | − 500,000 |
| III | Increase services | + 20,000,000 |
| IV | Develop new technology | + 500,000 |
| V | Increase housing | + 500,000 |
|  | Communications, transportation | + 1,600,000 |
| VI | Expand government | + 1,600,000 |
| VII | The arts | + 100,000 |
| First recapitulation total |  | + 23,800,000 |

Thus, all the conventional ways to expand employment will probably produce less than 24 million new jobs by the year 2005, leaving the country at least 16 million jobs

Recapitulation

short of the desired full employment level. What can we do to close the gap? One way would be to remove the present anti-employment bias of the tax system.

ENCOURAGING EMPLOYMENT

How a government raises its revenues through taxation can have a significant effect on total employment as well as influence the way in which the employment is divided between the various sectors of the economy. Two types of taxes in particular affect employment—those taxes levied directly on the payroll and those taxes and non-tax expenses that are levied based on the number of employees. Payroll taxes include Social Security, Medicare, unemployment insurance, and workman's compensation. Although not now financed through the tax system, health-care costs are determined by premiums based on the number of employees, regardless of their wages or salaries. Both these tax and health-care-premium costs provide a strong incentive to employers to reduce the hiring of new employees. *Business Week* magazine recently reported that for a business hiring a new worker at the minimum wage of $4.25 per hour, annual non-wage employee costs, sometimes known as "fringe benefits," now are as large as the wage payments— both are approximately $9,000 per year.[1] In business terms, the payroll loading is 100 percent. This obviously is a disincentive to hiring.

Further, the system of raising revenue through payroll taxes penalizes businesses with a high labor content as compared with those with high material costs. Payroll taxes and health-care premiums provide a strong incentive for labor-saving improvements that eliminate jobs.

There is no economic principle decreeing that these payroll taxes must exist. In Canada, both the costs of Social Security and health care are financed through the nation's income-tax system. Most European countries also rely on income and consumption taxes for revenue, rather than on

## CHAPTER VIII

payroll taxes. Thus, this book proposes that the United States change its payroll tax and health-care financing systems in two ways that would encourage employment, and particularly employment in the service sector:

1. Eliminate payroll taxes (both for employer and employee) for Social Security, Medicare, workman's compensation, and unemployment insurance on all wages and salaries of those with adjusted gross incomes below $30,000 per year (indexing this figure for inflation). Adjust the rates on salaries above that figure (with no upper limit) to produce the same revenue as the present taxes.

    A rough estimate of the effect of this proposed change can be made by looking at an analysis of income-tax returns for the year 1990.[2] In that year, out of the total wages and salaries reported of $2.5 trillion, $638 billion was earned by those with adjusted gross incomes of less than $30,000. The Social Security component of the FICA payroll tax is 6.2 percent each for employer and employee; 12.4 percent of $638 billion is $79 billion—income to the government which would be eliminated by the proposed change. At present, the liability for Social Security stops at $57,000. For simplicity, let's assume it stops at $50,000, since this is the figure available in the tax analysis. Those with adjusted gross incomes of more than $50,000 had wages and salary income in 1990 of $1.16 trillion. To compensate for the tax income lost by eliminating Social Security taxes on those with adjusted gross incomes of less than $30,000 would require an additional 6.8 percent ($79 billion divided by $1.16 trillion x 100) tax on wages and salaries of those with adjusted gross incomes of more than $50,000, presumably 3.4 percent each for employer and employee. Since the lower-paid worker is now expected to pay a tax of 6.2 percent, a tax at approximately one-half of that level on the salaries of the well-to-do does not seem unreasonable. Medicare, workman's compensation, and unemployment insurance premiums could be handled in the same way by

## Recapitulation

increasing the taxes on wages and salaries of those earning more than $50,000, who can well afford them.

Although the above calculations are based on adjusted gross income levels of less than $30,000, it probably would be easier to administer the taxes if the cutoff depended only on salaries and wages.

2. Finance health-care costs of those with an adjusted gross income of less than $30,000 from a new value-added tax (usually abbreviated to VAT), instead of from employer-paid insurance premiums that are calculated on the basis of numbers of employees. To tilt consumer demand toward services rather than goods, services would be exempt from this tax.

Again, a rough estimate can be made of the level of VAT that would be required to replace an employer's present insurance costs for health care for this group of employees. In 1990, 51.5 million income tax returns were filed by those with adjusted gross incomes of less than $30,000.[3] In 1992, when health-care costs had risen, employer health insurance costs averaged $1.02 per hour worked by employees, or $2,040 per year for a full-time employee.[4], Accordingly, health care for this group of taxpayers cost employers about $105 billion (51.5 million x $2,040). This is a very rough estimate since some of the returns were joint returns, and some of the employers did not provide health insurance. Personal consumption expenditures for durable and nondurable goods in 1992 totaled about $1.5 trillion.[5] Thus, a VAT to cover the medical costs of this group of employees through a tax on goods but not services would have had to be at a level of 7.0 percent ($105 billion divided by $1.5 trillion x 100). This is well below the level of the VAT in many European countries.

As in the case of payroll taxes, for ease of administration, this change probably should apply to all those with earnings from wages and salaries of less than $30,000, rather than making the cutoff dependent on gross income.

## CHAPTER VIII

If the present employer-financed health-care system is continued, the employer health-care costs for all employees in this salary range could be a direct credit against the employer's income taxes. If the final health-care plan approved by Congress shifts the health insurance burden to individual taxpayers, the insurance costs for those earning less than $30,000 could be a direct credit against their income taxes.

Both of these suggested changes would have the effect of reducing the costs of hiring new entry-level employees in both the goods and services sectors. Of course, since service industries are more labor intensive than manufacturing industries, the service sector would end up proportionally better off. As mentioned above, because the VAT would be levied on goods but not on services, there also should be a shift in consumer demand away from goods toward services, providing a further stimulus to employment in the service sector.

Both proposed changes in the tax laws also involve a different philosophy of taxation than that presently followed. Social Security is now regarded as sort of an insurance program, in which the payments by the worker and the employer go toward providing the retirement benefits of the worker. In practice, there is no direct relationship between the premiums and the benefits. At present, most retirees can expect to collect substantially more than they have paid into the system. Further, those who can best afford to pay a payroll tax are exempted from the Social Security tax on all of their salary over $57,000, whereas even the minimum-wage worker has to pay a Social Security tax of 6.2 percent of wages. (For Medicare, the payroll tax is 1.45 percent on wages up to $135,000.) As shown in the calculation above, the same total taxes on Social Security and Medicare could be collected by eliminating the top limit on the salaries that are taxed. The result of this change is that Social Security would no longer be considered an insurance program but

## Recapitulation

rather a "safety net" to provide for everyone in their retired years. This is the philosophy followed in most industrial countries.

The proposed change in financing health care also involves a shift from considering health care as an insurable risk that should be paid for by the employer to considering health care as a general right similar to education that should be financed by the government out of a new VAT for all those in the lower-income group. The individual employer would be reimbursed through credits against income taxes for premiums for health insurance for these lower-paid employees. Since his costs would be less, the employer could reduce his prices, and in most cases competition would force the employer to do so. Thus, the ultimate cost to the consumer of the product, including VAT, should be approximately the same. Of course, this would vary from business to business. If, as many believe, the health-care plan proposed by President Clinton will be substantially modified before it is implemented, this proposal could be incorporated in the final plan.

A value-added tax is a tax on each stage of production of goods and services, which ends up being a sort of sales tax. Unlike the income tax, the consumer feels that he or she has some control over whether the tax is paid, since it can be avoided simply by not purchasing the goods or services in question. Some economists see the VAT as a better way to raise revenue than the income tax because the VAT tends to discourage consumption and encourage savings.

Like a sales tax, a VAT is inherently regressive; it takes a larger percentage of the income of the poor than of the wealthy. However, this regressiveness can be largely compensated for by exempting from the VAT essentials such as food and drugs.

For those industries that export their products, a VAT to finance health care has an additional advantage over the

## CHAPTER VIII

present health-benefits insurance system. The present employer costs for health care are built into the cost of the product. A VAT, on the other hand, is identifiably separate and can be rebated for export goods, making the products more competitive. This is done by most countries who use a VAT. In addition, the United States could charge a VAT on imports, further improving the competitive position of American industry.

The main advantage, however, in both the elimination of payroll taxes and the elimination of employer-paid health-care costs for those in the lower wage and salary brackets would be to encourage the hiring of new employees. An anti-hiring bias of the present tax system would be transformed into a pro-employment policy.

It is likely, however, that even with encouragement in hiring new employees, the desired 40 million new jobs will not appear without further changes. The possibility of solving the shortfall in jobs through shorter workweeks or shorter work lives will be considered in the next two chapters.

# Chapter IX

# EMPLOYMENT EFFECTS OF LIMITING YEARS OF WORK:

## Youth Corps and the Golden Years

According to the U.S. Department of Labor, the composition of the work force in 1990 and that projected for the year 2005 are as follows (in millions).[1]

| Age/Year | 16–19 | 20–64 | 65 and over |
| --- | --- | --- | --- |
| 1990 | 7.4 | 113.8 | 3.5 |
| 2005 | 8.8 | 137.9 | 4.1 |

Presumably, all of those jobs now performed by youths 16–19 years old and by those 65 years and older could be performed by those in the prime of life, ages 20–64. By restricting access to the job market to those aged 20–64 years, 13 million more jobs would be available for this group in 2005. Even if there were no changes in working hours per week, as proposed in the next chapter, changing the years of work would essentially solve the unemployment problem for those in the prime age group.

# CHAPTER IX

Politically, however, it would be difficult, if not impossible, to restrict jobs to those between the ages of 20 and 64. What may be possible, though, is to provide incentives that will make it more attractive for those in the younger and older age groups to drop out of the labor force.

In addition to creating more jobs for those 20 years old and older, reducing employment of 16-19 year-old youths would give society the opportunity to train them so that eventually they would be more productive members of the work force. At present, the highest percentage of unemployment is in this age group. Of the 6.8 million youth ages 16-19 in the work force in 1992, about 1.4 million (21 percent) were unemployed.[2]

The restriction of youth employment could be accomplished in two steps. The first would be to raise the age of mandatory schooling to 18 on a national basis, and at the same time restricting employment of those ages 16 and 17. This would ensure that most students completed high school, a minimum requirement to function effectively in today's economy. Of course, remaining in school until age 18 does not guarantee a high school diploma, but it makes it more likely. In most states, the present minimum age for leaving school at 16 (age 14 in some) is a relic of nineteenth century rural America. Eight or ten years of education may have been sufficient for a prospective farmer 100 years ago; it is no longer sufficient in the computer age, even for one expecting to make a living in agriculture. Removing the 16- and 17-year-old youths from the work force would open up 3.6 million jobs in 2005 for those in the prime years of working life.[3]

The next step would be to encourage national service for those ages 18 and 19. Although such a program would be voluntary, if sufficiently attractive this could make up to 5.1 million additional jobs available for older workers in the year 2005. A national youth corps has been proposed from time to time since 1910, when William James wrote his

## Employment Effects of Limiting Years of Work

essay "The Moral Equivalent of War," in which he proposed that American youth be conscripted into "an army enlisted against nature."[4] A number of Presidents, including Woodrow Wilson, Franklin D. Roosevelt, Harry Truman, Dwight Eisenhower, John F. Kennedy, Lyndon Johnson, and Jimmy Carter have supported some sort of national youth corps. Most proposals would have allowed the young person to choose between military service and civilian community service in such fields as education, health care, and environmental preservation.

A typical suggestion is that made by Charles C. Moskos in his book *A Call to Civic Service*.[5] Moskos suggests a voluntary program involving one million young people a year, of whom 400,000 would serve in the military and 600,000 in civilian service. Those in the civilian corps could have the choice of a variety of jobs filling society's needs while not displacing paid workers in existing jobs. These might include:

1. Day Care
The youth volunteers would provide a pool of trainees who would complement the professional day-care staff. This would give more attention to the children, while keeping the costs of day care at an affordable level.

2. Service to the Aged
At the other end of the age spectrum are the elderly. It is forecast that there will be more than 4 million Americans over the age of 85 by the year 2010. Almost half of them will require some kind of care. Many of those who otherwise would require nursing-home care could remain at home if youth volunteers were available to help with errands, light housekeeping, and accompanied exercise.

# CHAPTER IX

3. Conservation

Those youths interested in conservation could help in construction and maintenance in national and state parks as well as in such traditional conservation functions as forestry.

In Moskos' proposal, volunteering would be made more attractive by linking it to scholarship aid for the volunteers. Moskos suggests that eventually participation in national service be made a prerequisite of receiving federal educational or vocational aid, such as student loans. A start toward such a program was taken in 1993 when Congress passed the National Youth Service Act.

An interesting variation on national service for all citizens age 18 and over was proposed by Richard Danzig and Peter Szanton in their 1986 book, *National Service: What Would It Mean?*[6] Their "universal service" requires one year of national service by all citizens age 18 or over, which could be performed at any time during a person's life. The program would be financed by a 5 percent surcharge on the income tax of anyone who had not previously performed the service. This surcharge would also provide the prod to service. The authors estimate that when fully implemented the program would attract 1.8 million participants. The largest cohort would be those 18 and 19 years old, but others could delay their service to later years. At whatever age, these participants would be in positions, like those in the Moskos proposal above, that did not eliminate existing jobs. By their participation, however, these universal service participants would open up jobs they otherwise would have held that would be filled by those in their prime work years.

In either the Moskos or the Danzig/Szanton proposal, volunteers could be supervised by a private nonprofit agency rather than by the government. This would utilize •the managerial skills of the nonprofits and minimize government bureaucracy. Examples of existing agencies that could be expanded to fill this function are the Student Conservation

## Employment Effects of Limiting Years of Work

Association, which matches young people with an interest in conservation with volunteer jobs in the national parks and forests, and Habitat for Humanity, which uses volunteers (including former President Jimmy Carter) to construct low-cost housing.

In addition to youths under age 20. another group that might be discouraged from continuing in the labor force are those who continue working after age 65. These older citizens now total 3.5 million, projected to rise to 4.1 million by the year 2005.[7] As noted in Appendix B, one of the reasons that the Japanese have such a low unemployment rate is that retirement at age 55 is customary. It is unlikely that in the United States the usual retirement age will drop to 55 in the foreseeable future; in fact, it might be politically impossible even to legislate mandatory retirement at age 65. It should be possible, however, to remove those restrictions that now prevent private employers from establishing a policy of mandatory retirement at age 65 if they wish. Further, the proposal to delay Social Security payments by penalizing retirement before age 67 should not be enacted if we want to encourage full employment in the prime working years. A national policy of discouraging employment after age 65 might reduce by half the number of those now projected to be working in their golden years in 2005, creating about 2 million job slots for younger workers.

Any move to restrict employment either of youth or of those over age 65 probably would be opposed by industry. Youth represents a pool willing to work at a minimum wage, often part-time with no benefit costs. With senior citizens, continuing to work after age 65 reduces the employers' pension liabilities and thus the required pension funding. However, the societal benefits of having full employment in the prime years of life would seem to outweigh this parochial attitude. Moreover, the nation needs

## CHAPTER IX

full employment in the 20-65 year age group to pay the taxes to support both young and old, rather than having those unemployed in the prime years themselves require welfare payments.

## Chapter X

# EMPLOYMENT EFFECTS OF LIMITING HOURS OF WORK:

## The Five-Day Weekend Revisited

*U*ntil the Second World War, the long-term trend in the United States was to reduce the hours worked per week. In 1820 the average worker spent from 12 to 15 hours each day on the job, 6 days a week—for a total workweek of between 72 and 90 hours. An early objective of the workingmen's parties was to reduce the workday to 10 hours, a goal first realized in 1836 when the Secretary of the Navy established a 10-hour day for the Philadelphia Navy Yard. By the time of the Civil War, the 10-hour day was the norm for skilled workers, although unskilled labor often worked longer hours.

The next goal, an 8-hour day, was also first reached with federal government employees when Congress passed an 1869 law limiting the hours for federally employed mechanics and laborers to 8. The Brotherhood of Carpenters, under the leadership of Peter McGuire, won an 8-hour day for its members in the building trade in 1890. Industry, however, strongly opposed shorter hours, often using violent tactics such as the employment in 1892 of Pinkerton guards to put down a strike at a Carnegie steel plant in Homestead,

# CHAPTER X

Pennsylvania. It took the First World War to bring the 8-hour day generally to industrial plants. Nevertheless, the 6-day workweek remained the norm until 1938, when Congress passed the Fair Labor Standards Act providing for a 44-hour week with a provision that the standard weekly hours should drop to 40 in 1941. Since 1941, the standard workweek has remained at this 40-hour level.[1]

Similar changes in working hours occurred in Europe during the late nineteenth and early twentieth centuries. In contrast to the United States, though, the reduction in working hours continued in Europe after the Second World War. The Europeans also increased the average vacations and holidays enjoyed by workers each year. The following table compares average workweeks and days off per year for vacations and holidays in various countries in 1991:[2]

| Country | Average Hours per Week | Average Days Off per Year |
|---|---|---|
| United States | 40 | 23 |
| France | 39 | 35 |
| Britain | 38.8 | 31 |
| Germany | 37.6 | 42 |

When other benefits such as paid sick leave and paid child-care leave are included, the average German worker spends almost 20 percent fewer hours on the job each year than his or her U.S. counterpart (1,480 hours per year in Germany compared with 1,847 in the United States). The German worker has not acquired this extra leisure at the cost of lower wages; the average hourly compensation of German workers, including benefits, is $24.36 compared to $15.39 in the United States.[2]

There also is a movement in France to spread the work by shortening the workweek to 4 days totaling 33 hours. A consultant, Pierre Larrouturou, has proposed that

## Employment Effects of Limiting Hours of Work

the new schedule start in 1996. Employers would maintain their profitability through wage cuts and elimination of the costs of unemployment insurance. Employees would be given a profit-sharing scheme that would eventually compensate for the wage cuts. The government would make up for the loss of unemployment insurance premiums through the reduced cost of unemployment benefits. Employment would rise by at least 10 percent and employees would have more free time. According to the *New York Times*, a majority in the French parliament now backs the idea of a shorter workweek.[3]

It is obvious that if the average employee spends fewer hour on the job, more employees will be required to accomplish the same amount of work. The effect is large. If the whole civilian labor force of the United States reduced its working hours by 20 percent, 30 million more jobs would be created by the year 2005, when the work force is projected to reach 150 million. .

Steps in this direction have been proposed from time to time in the last fifteen years. In 1979 Representative John Conyers of Michigan introduced H.R. 1784, a bill that would have changed the Fair Labor Standards Act of 1938 by setting a 35-hour standard workweek. In a letter to his committee, Conyers wrote, "We ought to look at reducing the working week and spreading employment among a greater number of workers, once again, as a means of reducing joblessness without sacrificing productivity."[4] The bill, however, died in committee.

In fact, the trend in the United States has been toward <u>longer</u> hours. A recent *New York Times* article stated that in April 1993 the average factory worker put in 4.3 hours of overtime. A major reason employers resort to overtime rather than hiring more workers is that health-care costs are a fixed amount per employee. Labor unions also like the overtime pay. The *Times* article points out that changing health-care financing either to a payroll tax or to a

71

## CHAPTER X

plan financed from general revenue would make employers more willing to hire new people.[5]

The trend to longer hours is not confined to factory workers. An earlier *New York Times* article reported that in 1991 nearly half of male executives, administrators, and managers worked 49 or more hours per week. The same *Times* article on this phenomenon quoted Robert E. Kutscher of the Bureau of Labor Statistics as saying, "We may be getting more throughput but no more output."[6]

The first step in resuming the trend toward shorter working hours might be for the government to mandate a 35-hour week for <u>federal</u> employees. This could be followed by requiring time-and-a-half overtime payments for work of more than 35 hours per week in any firm engaged in interstate commerce. If productivity continues to increase, firms could afford to increase the hourly rate to compensate for the shorter hours, leaving workers with the same take-home pay and more leisure time. Richard Freemen, a Harvard University economist, has suggested that a move to shorter hours might be cushioned by making jobless pay under the unemployment insurance program available to workers who agree to work only 30 instead of 40 hours per week at the same hourly wages. As mentioned above, switching to the European schedule of shorter workweeks and longer vacations could create as many as 30 million new jobs in the United States.

Shortening hours may not be costly to business providing the cost of fringe benefits is unlinked from the number of employees, as proposed in the previous chapter. Juliet B. Schor, an economist at Harvard, has stated that "shrinking the 40-hour workweek by up to five hours leads to less absenteeism, less turnover, less personal business on company time, and lower costs."[7]

In 1989 this author suggested a more radical solution to shortening hours and increasing jobs. In a book titled *The Five-Day Weekend,*[8] it was proposed that both the calendar

## Employment Effects of Limiting Hours of Work

and the workweek be changed to allow 5 days of work followed by a 5-day weekend. The first step would be to change to a fixed calendar so that the same day of the month would always fall on the same weekday. The calendar then would be further altered to 72 5-day weeks each year, grouped in 12 months of 6 weeks each, plus 5 holidays. This would be accompanied by a change in the work schedules so that while one employee was enjoying a long weekend a "job partner" would be doing the same job. In management situations the job partners would not be equals but rather one administrator and his or her assistant. The assistant would do the boss's job during the week that the boss was off, in the same way that the assistant now covers for the boss when the latter is away on a business trip or vacation. In those jobs for which the alternate workweek schedule is not suitable, other patterns such as working 3 days out of 5 could be substituted. This plan also has the potential for creating up to 30 million new jobs.

In contrast to simply reducing the workweek and adding vacations, the alternate-week work schedule would have the following advantages:
1. It would allow industrial and service firms to operate continuously, thus increasing their capacity and utilization of their assets.
2. Two-parent families with young children could arrange their schedules so that one parent is always at home with the children. This would allow the father to share the burdens of child care and housekeeping equally with the mother, to the advantage of both.
3. A switch of elementary and high schools to the alternate-week system would double the capacity of school buildings and still maintain 180 days of school per year.
4. Government services would become more accessible to the public since their offices would be open continuously.
5. The employee would have more leisure time for sports, hobbies, travel, and cultural and intellectual development.

# CHAPTER X

6. The leisure time could also be used for voluntary charitable activities as well as increased education that would produce a better-informed electorate.

I recognize, however, that the 7-day week is so ingrained in our social structure that changing the week to 5 days would be difficult. The European solution of shorter workweeks and more vacations probably is politically more feasible. Whichever path is chosen to shorten the workweek, shorter hours would not only reduce unemployment but also would give those who already have secure jobs more time for life outside of work.

## Chapter XI

## CONQUERING THE FEAR OF LEISURE

*T*he previous chapters demonstrated that the number of jobs could be increased either by decreasing the number of working hours per week or the number of working years in a worker's lifetime. In either case, the result would be more leisure for the individual worker.

This increased leisure is important not only to create jobs by means of job sharing in one of the modes previously mentioned but also to provide the time required for people to consume the services necessary to sustain the economy.

Americans have an ambivalent feeling toward leisure. Most working people look forward to vacations and weekends. Yet surveys show that whenever they are given a choice to do whatever they want in their free time, they feel that the result is dull and unsatisfying. The American Association for the Advancement of Psychiatry published a study about forty years ago that concluded that "leisure is dangerous for most Americans."[1]

A number of leaders have tried to change this fear of leisure. In the 1920s and 1930s, Monsignor John A. Ryan, a leader of the social-reform wing of the Roman Catholic Church, wrote extensively on the need for shorter working hours in order to obtain time for the enjoyment of "the

## CHAPTER XI

higher goods of life."[2] Abba Hillel Silver, president of the Central Conference of American Rabbis, wrote that increased leisure would provide time for learning, for culture, for individual creativity, and for the appreciation of life.[3] A Canadian professor of political economy, Stephen Leacock, also well known as a humorist, endorsed the shorter workweek as a way to allow workers to enjoy culture, music and friends. He wrote that the whole point of human progress might very well be to give everyone enough free time to watch the sun set.[4]

Of course, increased leisure time could be spent watching even more television, which William Bennett, former Secretary of Education and a fellow at the Heritage Foundation, recently reported in *The Wall Street Journal* averaged more than seven hours each day for adult Americans in 1992.[5] For many viewers. television provides an opportunity to learn about nature and keep up with world affairs. Some of this time, however, might more profitably be spent in active, rather than passive, learning. As Dorothy Canfield Fisher pointed out in the early 1930s, we are facing

> a totally new phase of human life, in which education must achieve in fact what has been its true purpose all along—individual growth in the thin new element of intellectual and artistic activities and of abstract thought...It is now apparent that what is needed is not at all a mere extension to more people of the kind of education that used to be given to boys and girls under twenty-one years of age, but rather nothing less than the development of a method by which persons of all ages can be taught to substitute spontaneous intellectual effort for enforced material effort.[6]

The increased use of community colleges and other educational facilities for adult education by those having new

## Conquering the Fear of Leisure

leisure to take the courses should increase employment of teachers and support personnel.

Of course, leisure can be used for physical as well as intellectual development. Eventually there will be at least five more hours a week for bowling or tennis—or to spend at the local fitness center. For those more interested in spectator sports, the increased leisure time could be spent watching baseball or horse racing. Employment of those conducting all of these activities should increase accordingly.

Others will use their new free time for cultural activities. There should be increased attendance at natural history and art museums, at musical comedies and operas, and at symphony and country-and-western concerts. For those who have the talent and inclination, the time can be spent in learning to play the accordion or in participating in a barber shop quartet.

The travel industry also would benefit. If the United States adopts the European six-week vacation as standard, families and individuals will travel more at home and abroad. The economic beneficiaries will include travel agents, airlines, hotels, and destination resorts and amusement facilities.

Some people will choose to use their new leisure for voluntary community service or charitable activities. Many of these organizations have suffered a severe loss of volunteer help as women who were formerly volunteers have entered the work force either full time or part-time. Many volunteer fire departments and volunteer ambulance corps are desperate for more female fire fighters and ambulance drivers. The Red Cross, the Salvation Army, as well as churches, synagogues, and mosques, all need more volunteer help—both male and female. In addition to the satisfaction derived by the volunteers in helping a worthy cause, their support will also eventually lead to more employment by the central offices of these organizations.

## CHAPTER XI

There is no shortage of interesting and useful ways to spend increased leisure time. One can even write and publish books, as this author has done! Increased leisure can also add to the _quality_ of life by allowing more time to be with one's family and friends and to help neighbors. Life might become more similar to the fondly remembered life-style of the nineteenth century.

As Dorothy Canfield Fisher pointed out, however, Americans will have to be taught that time spent on leisure activities is as important as time spent in the work place. It may take a new generation of young people before the majority accept that work is a means to an end, not an end in itself, and that the desirable result of work includes not only the ability to buy possessions but also the leisure time for both intellectual development and amusement.

In deciding whether or not it would be better to seek more leisure rather than more consumer goods, it might be worth pondering the lyrics of a popular song of the 1930s[7]:

> Are you havin' any fun?
> What ya gettin' out of living?
> What good is what you've got
> If you're not
> Havin' any fun?
>
> Better have a little fun.
> You ain't gonna live forever.
> Before you're old and gray,
> Still okay, have a little fun, son,
> Have a little fun!

## Chapter XII

# FIRST PRECONDITION FOR FULL EMPLOYMENT:

## An Educated Work Force

*I*n the previous two chapters we have explored proposals for creating jobs in the private sector by shortening hours of work or years in the labor force. As mentioned previously, this approach is an alternative to achieving full employment by having the government become the employer of last resort, as was done during the New Deal in the 1930s. Even if the jobs are to be provided primarily by the private sector, however, the government has a very important role to play in establishing two preconditions required for the private sector to do its part. The first of these preconditions, an educated work force, is far from being met. For example, in 1987 the New York Telephone Company undertook its first major recruiting effort in more than a decade. Applicants were tested for skills including vocabulary, number relationships, and problem-solving abilities for entry-level jobs ranging from telephone operator to service representative. Out of the first 22,880 applicants, 84 percent failed the tests. This is not an isolated case. A New York City bank reported that only 15 out of every 500

# CHAPTER XII

candidates tested and interviewed on a weekly basis were hired for the entry-level job of bank teller.[1]

In the future, educational requirements for most entry-level jobs will be more demanding than they are now. The Hudson Institute estimates that by the year 2000, 87 percent of new jobs will require the completion of four years of high school, with 55 percent of these new jobs requiring at least some college education.[2]

Both now and in the future the twin problems of education and employment are especially acute among minority youth in the inner cities. According to the National Urban League, the unemployment rate for black youths in poor areas is 60 percent.[3] As mentioned in the previous chapter, the Bureau of Labor Statistics counts as unemployed only those actively looking for work, so the official reported unemployment rates are lower. Still, nationwide for black high-school dropouts age sixteen to twenty-four, the Bureau of Labor Statistics showed in the year 1991 a 48 percent unemployment rate.[4]

There are a number of programs and proposals for reducing the high-school dropout rate and improving the performance of graduates. These include turning the inner-city public schools over to private contractors and providing parents with vouchers that could be used for either public or private schools. Although many of these programs have shown promise in demonstration projects, there is as yet no nationwide consensus on these radical changes.

There is, however, broad agreement that equipping all Americans with the skills needed for employment in the twenty-first century requires preparation for learning starting in the very young years. Because of the prevalence of single-parent families in which the single parent works full time outside the home and two-parent families in which both parents are employed outside the home, this preparation in most cases no longer occurs at home. Optimally, this early learning takes place in a day care setting, with trained teachers. But only one-third of American three- and four-year-olds attend preschools or day-care centers. In contrast, 99 percent of French three-, four-. and five-year olds attend preschool at no or minimal charge.

The French also have a comprehensive system of care for children between three months and three years of age, Day-care centers, or *crèches*, operate from 7 A.M. to 7 P.M. and are heavily subsidized, with poor families paying only $390 per year. As an alternative, there are day-care homes run by government-licensed baby-sitters who must pass rigid medical and psychological tests and whose homes must also meet government standards. The facilities are so good that even affluent French parents, who used to keep their children home with nannies, now use *crèches* or day-care homes to give their children the advantage of socialization.[5]

In the United States, the Head Start program has been remarkably successful in providing this preparation for those segments of society not able to afford private nursery schools. However, it reaches less than half the eligible children, and there is no provision to extend the program to two- and three-year-olds. Eventually, Head Start or its equivalent should be available to all children.

There also is broad agreement that elementary and secondary education in mathematics and the sciences must be improved. In the late 1980s, tests were given to high-school students in thirteen countries. In these tests, U.S. students placed ninth in physics, eleventh in chemistry, and at the very bottom in biology.[6] A 1992 report issued by the Organization for Economic Cooperation and Development was somewhat more encouraging and elicited the headline "International Report Card Shows U.S. Schools Doing the Job" over a *New York Times* article on the report. The statistics accompanying the article, however, showed that the United States still ranked ninth out of ten industrialized countries in performance of its students in mathematics.[7]

## CHAPTER XII

Partly as a result of the earlier survey, President George Bush convened the nation's governors to discuss ways to improve U.S. students' academic performance. The governors in March 1990 established six national educational goals, later backed by the President. According to the goals, students must demonstrate proficiency in mathematics, science, history and other subjects. Further, a goal was established of leading the world in mathematics and science by the year 2000.[8]

A debate is currently underway on measuring progress toward meeting the goal of demonstrated proficiency. President Bush pushed for national student standards, and President Bill Clinton early in his term proposed federal legislation to oversee work on developing standards and assessments. This initiative, however, has aroused fears that assessments and standards would, in effect, require a standard national curriculum, similar to those used in France, Germany, and Japan. Such a national curriculum would, of course, greatly reduce the authority of local school boards. Further, comparative tests would highlight the differences between the performance of students in affluent school districts and poor ones, increasing the pressure for equalization of resources.[9] Nevertheless, the success of a national curriculum in the schools of our international competitors seems likely to push the United States in this direction.

Edward Luttwak in his book *The Endangered American Dream* has suggested giving extra federal pay to teachers who can pass uniform qualifying examinations administered on a nationwide basis. He also would reward students who passed specified national educational achievement tests with a federal diploma.[10]

A further suggestion for improving the performance of American students is to lengthen the school year. In the United States, 175 to 180 school days each year is normal. The equivalent schedule in Western Europe is 200 days or more, with 220 days standard in Japan and South Korea. By the age of eighteen, the average Japanese or Korean child will have had the equivalent of three or four years more education than John and Mary in the United States. Our present school schedule is really a carryover from the days when children were needed to help their parents plant and harvest the crops and has little justification now that farm families are less than 2 percent of the population.[11]

The United States also can learn from its competitors in providing apprenticeship programs for high-school graduates. In Germany, approximately 65 percent of middle-school graduates enter apprenticeship programs. The fields range from laundress and chimney sweep to skilled mechanic and secretary. The apprenticeships involve both practical and theoretical training; the laundress might be required to write a paper on the theory of detergents and the chimney sweep on the theory of combustion. In 1984, the program trained more than 1.7 million young people. The costs are borne jointly by government and industry. In addition, employers and the government jointly pay tuition for off-hours education in state-supported schools to train existing workers in new technology.[12]

The National Center on Education and the Economy, based in Rochester, New York, recently published a study proposing an Americanized version of the German apprentice system. The study proposes that all students acquire basic academic skills by the age of sixteen, at which time they would pass tests measuring their ability to read, write, and compute at world-class levels. Those who failed the test would attend youth centers for remedial training. Students then could choose a college-bound path or a vocational path. Those choosing the vocational path would participate from two to four years in a work-study program, attending high schools, community colleges, or technical schools while working part-time for local firms. Those in the vocational path would still be free to change their minds and transfer into four-year colleges.[13]

# CHAPTER XII

For those who choose to go on to college, scholarships and other forms of financial aid should be available so that ability to learn rather than ability to pay becomes the basis for college admission. The Education Act of 1993, which provides financial aid that may be repaid through community service, is a good start in this direction.

Finally, preparation for jobs in the twenty-first century cannot stop with completion of an apprenticeship program or graduation from college or university. Learning should continue during each worker's career to master new skills and technologies as they are developed. This process can be encouraged by the federal and state governments through generous tax deductions both to individuals and corporations for the costs of lifetime learning.

The need to improve the quality of elementary and secondary education and to provide for lifetime learning was underscored by a study released by the U.S. Department of Education in September 1993. The study found that nearly half of the adults in this country were not proficient enough in English to write a letter about a billing error or to use a bus schedule to calculate the length of a trip. The study measured five levels of proficiency. Based on a random sample, it found that nearly 44 million Americans were unable to perform at the lowest level, which involved such simple tasks as determining the difference in price between two items or filling out an employment form. The tests indicated that an additional 40 million people could not perform at the second lowest level, which involved answering questions about the content of a newspaper story or writing a short paragraph summarizing information on a chart about schools.[14]

Obviously, it does no good to create jobs unless there are qualified applicants to fill them. Furthermore, the very process of improving education, from Head Start to adult literacy training, in itself creates a substantial number of teaching and administrative positions.

## Chapter XIII

# SECOND PRECONDITION FOR FULL EMPLOYMENT:

## A Sound Economy

To achieve full employment, the United States will need not only an educated work force but also a sound economy. As in the case of education, this second precondition is necessary but not sufficient. The economy could be in a state that most economists would consider sound but still have substantial unemployment. In fact, as discussed in the introductory chapter and in Appendix A, many economists believe that there must be substantial unemployment in order for the economy to avoid excessive inflation.

"Sound" is a non-quantitative adjective for an area, economics, that the economists love to quantify. Although probably no two economists would agree completely on numerical criteria for a sound economy, a consensus probably could be reached along the following lines:

1. The total output of the economy, as measured by the Gross National Product, should be constant or increasing.

2. The balance in the current account between the United States and the rest of the world, which includes both trade

# CHAPTER XIII

in goods and services and financial factors such as dividend payments, should be neutral or positive.

3. The value of the currency should be constant or decrease in value at a rate of no more than 3 percent each year.

4. The government deficit as a percentage of the GNP should be constant or decrease from year to year.

In addition to these four criteria for soundness of the economy, many people would add a fifth:

5. The income distribution should be such that the gap in the share of national income between the richest and the poorest segments of the population stays constant or decreases rather than increases as it has done since 1980.

Before discussing the effect of these criteria on employment, we shall briefly review two examples of classical economic thinking on unemployment. Students still study Say's Law, an economic analysis that led to the conclusion that overproduction is impossible because supply creates its own demand. This led to the further deduction that there should be no employment problem. The economist Paul Samuelson says that the French writer J.B. Say (who formulated his law in 1803) and his followers "had the notion that, if only the money wage would fall far enough, it would always bring out job offers for every willing worker."[1] This theory that overproduction is impossible and unemployment is not a problem was also subscribed to by such well-known classical economists as David Ricardo, John Stuart Mill, and Alfred Marshall. Samuelson reports that as late as 1933 the classical economist A.C. Pigou wrote, "Such unemployment as exists at any time is due wholly to the frictional resistances that prevent the appropriate wage and price adjustments being made simultaneously."[2] Since at that time the unemployment rate in the United States was approaching 25 percent, the economic model based on the Say/Pigou theory did not correspond at all closely with reality.

Sound Economy

A similar problem of lack of correspondence between theory and reality has afflicted many of the economic theories since then that included unemployment in their model. There was much discussion thirty years ago of the Phillips Curve, named after A.W. Phillips of the London School of Economics. The Phillips Curve was a graph relating annual wage and price changes to average unemployment. It showed that as unemployment increased, inflation went down. Professor Phillips found that British historical data between 1861 and 1957 fell neatly on his curve. He concluded that to hold wage rates stable (and thus avoid cost-push inflation) required an unemployment rate of about 5 1/2 percent.[3] When this approach was applied to different economies and different time periods, economists found that there was not just one curve but a whole family of curves. Currently, most economists no longer speak of the Phillips Curve but rather pick a single figure for what they call the "non-accelerating rate of unemployment," or NAIRU.[4] This figure also varies from country to country and from time to time within a country. Thus, the NAIRU concept is not a very useful guide to employment policy.

Let us now return to the criteria for a sound economy.
GROSS NATIONAL PRODUCT

The Gross National Product (GNP) is a statistic compiled by the Department of Commerce of the sum of personal expenditures for goods and services, private capital expenditures such as new homes and new industrial plants, government purchases, and export balance. It has limitations in that it does not measure the social value of the goods and services produced (cigarettes and liquor count the same as education expenses), nor does it take into account how the goods and services are distributed among the population.[5] Further, there is no direct correlation between the GNP and employment. These limitations are discussed further in the next chapter.

# CHAPTER XIII

However, GNP is the simplest measurement of overall economic activity. Large changes in the GNP obviously effect employment, as witnessed by the Great Depression. Full employment certainly requires that the GNP not decrease.

In trying to manage the economy to produce an even growth of the GNP, the government uses fiscal policies of increasing or decreasing government expenditures and taxes, as well as monetary policies of controlling the money supply and interest rates. Over the past twenty years, the relative importance of fiscal controls and monetary controls has shifted toward the monetarists. Neither sets of policies, however, has been completely successful. There is apparently a large psychological component in the purchasing habits of the consumer. A rough measure of consumer attitude is taken regularly with a "consumer confidence survey," but changing these attitudes is not simply a matter of adjusting tax rates and interest rates.

## BALANCE OF TRADE

In 1992 the United States imported nearly $100 billion more goods than it exported. Since imported goods provide jobs elsewhere, not here, a more even balance between imports and exports would provide more U.S. jobs. Fortunately, the negative trade balance in goods was partially offset in 1992 by a $70 billion favorable trade balance in services.[6] The aim of the government, of course, is to reduce the unfavorable balance in merchandise trade while preserving or increasing the balance of trade in services. It is not yet clear whether the conclusion of the recent trade negotiations on the North American Free Trade Agreement (NAFTA) and the General Agreement on Tariffs and Trade (GATT) will have this effect, but the administration obviously hopes so.

Sound Economy

INFLATION

Currency inflation, to the degree experienced in the past by the United States, has relatively little direct effect on employment. Prices rise, but wages do also. Inflation usually, but not always, is accompanied by an economic boom, which may actually increase employment. Of course, hyperinflation of the kind experienced in Germany after World War I and more recently in Latin America has a devastating effect on the economy and thus employment.

In the United States, though, the effect of inflation on employment has usually been caused by government action to combat inflation rather than by inflation per se. One mechanism for dampening inflation is to decrease consumer demand by purposely inducing a recession, either by raising interest rates or by restricting the growth of the money supply. The resulting recession invariably increases unemployment. The government hopes, naturally, that it can control inflation by use of these fiscal and monetary tools in moderation without having to induce a recession or depression.

An alternative to controlling inflation by inducing a recession is to impose price controls. These were very effective when introduced by President Harry Truman in 1950 at the time of the Korean War. Even after the removal of price controls by President Dwight Eisenhower in 1953, inflation continued at a rate of less than 3 percent for the next ten years.[7] The low inflation rate was broken not by full employment but by the shock of OPEC-induced price increases in crude oil. Most economists do not like price controls since they interfere with the operation of the market economy, but experience in the United States and elsewhere has shown that sometimes they can be effective in curbing inflation without creating unemployment.

## CHAPTER XIII

### GOVERNMENT DEFICIT

Of the first four components of a sound economy, a level or declining government deficit is probably the least important. The general public tends to equate the national debt with a family's debt, but the analogy is really a false one. As pointed out by the economists Robert Heilbroner and Lester Thurow, since most government bonds are held by U.S. citizens, the national debt is more comparable with one family member owing money to another member than to the family as a whole being in debt.[8] Further, Paul Samuelson and William Nordhaus point out that the U.S. debt as a percentage of GNP is comparable to what it has been historically and is less than it was in Britain during that country's century of growth prior to the First World War.[9]

Nevertheless, a large <u>external</u> debt with its consequent large interest payments to foreigners does place a burden on the economy. In countries like Brazil and Mexico the service of the external debt has been nearly ruinous. To the extent that the United States has financed its deficits by borrowing abroad, it has saddled future generations with costs that inevitably will reduce their standard of living below what it would have been if the payments to foreigners of interest and capital were not required. In the long run, this will adversely affect employment.

### INCOME DISTRIBUTION

In the United States in recent years, income distribution has been moving toward greater disparity rather than more equal distribution. As mentioned in the introductory chapter, the economist Paul Krugman has calculated that between 1979 and 1987 the real income before taxes of the top 10 percent of the population rose by 21 percent while that of the bottom 10 percent <u>declined</u> by 12 percent.[10] This trend seems to be continuing.

In addition to the moral question of whether it is just for a small segment of the population to receive a large

## Sound Economy

share of the national income, a more equal distribution would have a favorable effect on employment. As pointed out by George Brockway, the poor spend all of any additional income they can get, whereas the rich are already spending all that they can.[11] In other words, the greater the income disparity between the top and bottom, the fewer consumers there will be with the requisite purchasing power to favorably effect demand for goods and services. This is particularly important for services such as entertainment. In order to fill a 50,000-seat stadium, one must have 50,000 customers willing and able to pay $15 per ticket, providing a total of $750,000 spent on entertainment services. If the equivalent purchasing power is concentrated in one corporate executive mogul who already earns $5 million each year, he probably will use it to buy $750,000 in government bonds. If he does spend it, it will likely be to pay $750,000 for a diamond necklace for his wife. In either case, the stadium will be empty. If this occurs in a number of stadiums, there will be thousands of unemployed ball players, umpires, ticket sellers, grounds keepers, hot-dog vendors, and others who are dependent on spectator sports for employment. Of course, the diamond necklace provides employment for some South African diamond miners and Amsterdam diamond cutters, but it doesn't help U.S. employment.

Another important part of the service sector consists of the various repair shops, such as shoe repair, electrical-appliance repair, and furniture repair. People in the lower and middle classes usually prefer to fix a repairable article such as shoes or boots; the upper-class socialite will simply toss a pair of shoes with worn heels. Repairing an object rather than buying a new one not only provides service-sector employment but also helps the environment.

The two countries with the best records of full employment, Japan and Sweden, both have much more equal income distributions than we have in the United States. Japan and Sweden had unemployment rates below

# CHAPTER XIII

3.5 percent from 1970 through 1991.[12] In Japan, the ratio between the salary of the highest- and lowest-paid person in a corporation averages 17; in the United States the ratio in some corporations is more than 100.[13] Of course, the populations in both Sweden and Japan are more homogeneous that in the United States, but this does not have any direct relationship to income distribution.

At the other end of the scale, the vast income disparity existing in some developing countries such as Brazil is a major source of political and social unrest, which eventually affects the economy and employment. The United States income distribution is between that of Sweden and Brazil, but it is moving in the Brazilian direction. If there is continued movement in the direction of inequality, the resultant social unrest could eventually adversely affect our overall economy and employment as well as the stability of the government..

Although the government cannot do much about the distribution of income before taxes, it can have an effect on the distribution of after-tax income. A more steeply graduated income tax, although anathema to the rich, should help the economy, particularly if the higher receipts at the upper end of the scale are used to reduce the taxes of the middle and lower classes, leaving them with more purchasing power. The old argument that we needed to leave the rich with a large surplus to invest in new production facilities no longer seems valid in a service-oriented economy.

A recent book titled *The Maximum Wage*[14] proposes a radical solution to the problem of achieving a more equitable distribution of income—to limit the maximum wage to 10 times the minimum wage. If the annual income under a minimum wage of $4.00 per hour were $8,000 (from working 50 weeks of 40 hours each), the maximum wage would be $80,000. A person earning 5 times the minimum wage would be taxed at 5 percent and one earning $80,000 would be taxed at 10 percent. All income of more than

Sound Economy

$80,000 for an individual or $160,000 for a couple would be taxed at 100 percent. The author calculates that if this scheme had been in effect in 1990, all but the richest 1 percent of Americans would have paid less income taxes. A couple with an income of $125,000 would have paid only $8,800 in taxes, as compared with more than $20,000 under the 1990 tax code. The taxes on the very rich, however, would more than make up for the lower taxes on everyone else, producing a $175 billion increase in federal revenues, enough to erase most of the budget deficit. Such a radical change in the treatment of the very rich would be extremely difficult politically to accomplish, but the idea is intriguing.

The above discourse on the economy is a superficial glance at a very complex subject. Interested readers can find much further information in the books cited in the notes, such as the standard Paul Samuelson and William Nordhaus textbook on economics. For those readers with less time and perseverance than is required to study Samuelson, economists Robert Heilbroner and Lester Thurow have helpfully condensed and rewritten their economics textbook in a very readable book titled *Economics Explained*.

In any case, as stated in the opening paragraph of this chapter, maintaining a sound economy through gradual increase in the GNP, balancing our foreign trade, keeping inflation and the budget deficit under control, and working toward an equitable distribution of national income are steps that are <u>necessary</u> but not <u>sufficient</u> to reach full employment. The previous chapters have suggested additional steps that both the government and the private sector might take to reach this goal. After a brief digression to examine in more detail the limitations of using the Gross National Product growth alone as a measure of national well being, we shall summarize these recommendations.

## Chapter XIV

## THE GREAT GOD GNP

The conventional political and economic response to unemployment is to stimulate the economy by increasing government spending or reducing government taxes. The object of stimulation is to increase the growth of the GNP, which presumably will lead to more jobs. This chapter will focus on the limitations of this approach.

GNP stands for Gross National Product. The U.S. Department of Commerce defines GNP as "the market value of goods and services produced by labor and property supplied by U.S. residents." As long as the labor and property are supplied by U.S. residents, they can be located either in the United States or abroad. Although GNP is the term that is still popularly used, most economists now prefer Gross Domestic Product (GDP), which differs from GNP in that the labor and property used must be located in the United States. In the GDP measurement the workers can be foreign residents, such as foreign nationals employed by their home governments, and the property can be owned by foreigners.

GNP (or GDP) growth from quarter to quarter is the single statistic most watched by economists to determine the health of the economy. It is usually converted to an

## The Great God GNP

annual growth figure. Real (inflation-adjusted) annual GNP growths of less than 3 percent are considered anemic, whereas those of more than 5 percent are considered robust. Since the market value of goods and services is affected by inflation of the currency, growth figures are often presented in terms of constant-dollar GNPs. The fine print describing how this adjustment is made occupies several densely written paragraphs in the footnotes to the government tables, which I assume any reader who likes fine print will check.[1]

In any analysis of the economy, the GNP statistics are basic. The detailed breakdown of these figures to show which sectors of the economy are growing and which are decreasing have been used throughout this book. However, it is the single overall GNP figure which is quoted on the television news shows and is thus impressed on the mind of the general public. As a composite figure, though, the GNP measurement has some limitations that are not generally realized by the public.

In general, GNP measures the output of the economy by summing up all of the incomes. Yet, some important outputs have no corresponding reported incomes. The most important of these is unpaid domestic labor, principally housework. Although when one eats out, the wages of the chef and the waiter are included in the GNP, the corresponding labor if the meal is prepared at home is not recorded. Similarly, child care in a day-care center is recorded, but child care at home is not.[2]

Other income that does not show up in the GNP is that produced by barter, the simple exchange of goods or services, rather than by purchase with money. Activity in voluntary organizations and unpaid charitable activity also are excluded.

Because of the way it is calculated, GNP assigns no relative values to any of its components. One result is that disasters help to increase the GNP. For instance, hurricane

## CHAPTER XIV

Andrew's devastating effect in 1992 on south Florida led to large expenditures for rebuilding houses, stores, and public facilities—all of which added to the GNP. The 1993 explosion in the World Trade Center in New York City was a boon to the construction industry in that city. The AIDS epidemic has brought about greatly increased expenditures on hospital services in our major metropolitan areas; again, this is good for the GNP. Low-birth-weight babies, who may require $250,000 of care before they are able to survive independently, similarly contribute to growth in the GNP. Both the AIDS crisis and crack-related baby deaths have also increased the demand for caskets, another GNP component. On the other hand, decrease in the consumption of cigarettes or whiskey has a negative effect on the GNP. From a strictly economic point of view, the trends in consumption of tobacco and hard liquor are terrible. Further, the negative effect of these downward liquor and tobacco trends on the GNP is exacerbated by the fact that they also cause a decline in the consumption of caskets, at least in the short term.

The GNP measurements also obscure the distribution to various sectors of society of the products and services they record. As noted in the previous chapter, between 1979 and 1987 the real income before taxes of the top 10 percent of the population rose by 21 percent while that of the bottom 10 percent declined by 12 percent. During those same years, the GNP (in 1987 dollars) rose from 3.8 to 4.5 trillion dollars, which was 18 percent.[3] Even though the 1980s were growth years for the economy as a whole, the effect on those living in poverty was to make their lives even more miserable.

Especially pertinent to this book is the further fact that employment growth is not directly proportional to GNP growth. As noted above, between 1979 and 1987 the GNP adjusted for inflation increased by 18 percent. During those same years, total full-time employment grew from 82.7

million to 93.0 million, which is only 12.5 percent.[4] One reason for the lack of direct proportionality between GNP growth and employment growth is that productivity improvements reduce the amount of labor required per unit of GNP Further, different sectors of the economy have vastly different outputs per unit of labor input. For instance, those working in the manufacture of radios and television sets have three times the output of the workers in steel foundries. The output of workers in retail stores or in restaurants and hotels is even lower than of those in the foundries.[5] A growth in the proportion of the GNP produced by high-technology industries such as computers will produce fewer jobs than the growth in low-technology sectors such as beauty parlors and retail stores. Thus in looking at strategies for achieving full employment, one has to balance the fact that new types of jobs are more likely to come from the high-technology manufacturing sector but that an increase in the demand for services will produce _more_ jobs than the same increase in the demand for high-technology goods.

GNP growth also has no predictable relationship to whether the environment is being helped or harmed. In general, growth in the goods-producing sectors is more harmful to the environment than the same amount of growth in the service-producing sectors. To manufacture goods requires energy, which in most cases is derived from carbon sources such as coal or petroleum. Thus, carbon dioxide is produced, adding to the greenhouse effect. If the energy is produced by nuclear power, there is the problem of disposal of radioactive waste. Even hydroelectric power has deleterious environmental effects through the flooding of land in the impoundment areas behind the dams. Of course, the service sector also uses energy but proportionally less per unit of output. Obtaining the raw materials used in the manufacturing sector also adversely affects the environment. Open-pit mining to obtain copper, nickel, and iron produces ugly scars on the landscape, and the petroleum used as a raw material

## CHAPTER XIV

for plastics is the source of accidents such as the disastrous *Exxon Valdez* spill of crude oil at Prudhoe Bay in Alaska. Further, manufactured goods at the consumer level generally have multiple packaging, adding to the waste-disposal problem. Obviously, the service sector uses little in the way of raw materials or packaging.

A measurement closely allied to GNP is GNP per capita, which is the total amount of goods and services divided by the U.S. population. This figure is often equated with the standard of living. It suffers, however, from the same defects as the GNP statistic from which it is derived. As noted above, GNP makes no distinction between the social worth of the different economic activities it records. Over the past two decades, one major source of U.S. economic growth has been increased expenditures for national defense. Thus, although most people would not feel that their standard of living has been increased because their country built two more aircraft carriers and a new wing of strategic bombers, equating the standard of living to the GNP per capita purports to show just that. A similar purported increase in the standard of living may in fact be caused by sky-rocketing expenses in health care. The standard of living may appear to increase because the wealthy are receiving and spending a lot more money, the middle class income is unchanged, and the poor are getting poorer. In past years, a so-called increase in the standard of living also was often accompanied by smog in the air and pollution in the streams.

Finally, GNP does not record any value for leisure time. As previously noted, increased productivity in either the manufacturing or service sector can result either in increased production or more leisure time. Focusing on GNP growth biases the choice toward increased output rather than more leisure.

## The Great God GNP

Thus, neither GNP nor GNP per capita (standard of living) measurement reflects the social worth of the goods or services produced, does not indicate how the resulting income is distributed, does not directly correlate with employment, and does not reflect environmental concerns. If the Gross National Product is not the best way to monitor national progress, which measures should we pay attention to? What we really need is some measure of the satisfaction of human needs, which include:

1. Food, shelter, and clothing
2. Health care
3. A safe environment with clean air and clean water
3. Public safety and public order
4. Education and knowledge
5, Transportation and communication
6. Recreation and amusement

For each of the above needs, an index already exists or could easily be designed. For instance, the crime statistics measure public safety and statistics on clean air and water already compiled by the Environmental Protection Agency measure environmental safety. A number of other indicators are proposed by the British economist Victor Anderson in his book *Alternative Economic Indicators*.[6] These indices could then be weighted and combined in a composite Satisfaction of Human Needs (SHN) figure. How to establish and weight these indices would be grist for the doctoral-theses mill.

The government could then concentrate on maximizing the SHN rather than the GNP, as well as on ensuring that employment is available for all those who wish it. Employment and unemployment are, of course, already closely monitored, but I would suggest that in the future the emphasis be on the unemployment statistic that includes those working part-time who want full-time jobs as well as those who want to work but are not currently hunting for

## CHAPTER XIV

jobs. This latter figure is already calculated but not widely published by the Bureau of Labor Statistics of the Department of Labor.

## Chapter XV

## RECOMMENDATIONS AND CONCLUSIONS

*I*n Chapter VIII, Recapitulation, we concluded that conventional methods of increasing employment would produce about 24 million new jobs between 1992 and 2005, still leaving the United States in the year 2005 with 16 million less jobs than required for full employment.

In his book *The Zero-Sum Society,* the economist Lester Thurow states:

> We consistently preach that work is the only "ethical" way to receive income. We cast aspersions on the "welfare" society. Therefore we have a responsibility to guarantee full employment. Not to do so is like locking the church doors and then saying that people are not virtuous if they do not go to church.[1]

Thurow then proposes to guarantee jobs by having the federal government set up job programs in competition with private industry. He gives as an example the rebuilding of railway roadbeds in competition with private enterprise. He proposes that this federal program be structured to

# CHAPTER XV

provide earnings and promotional opportunities similar to those provided at present by private industry for white males. He believes that by proper project selection such a program would generate benefits in excess of its costs.

Like Thurow's proposal, most of the alternative approaches that have been suggested to achieve full employment involve creating <u>public-sector</u> jobs. Certainly, there is a lot of worthwhile work that could be done in the public sector, but there are two primary disadvantages to this approach. The first is cost. To create 16 million jobs at a minimum wage level of $9,000 per year would cost $144 billion in direct costs, plus at least $25 billion in administrative costs or nearly $170 billion in new taxes. Politically, this would be impossible. Further, experience with WPA jobs in the 1930s shows a stigma would be attached to working for the government on is perceived as "make-work" projects, even if they were of use to society as a whole. Thus, with the exception of a much smaller expenditure to encourage service in a youth corps, this book does not recommend that the government be the employer of last resort.

Instead, it proposes the creation of jobs by limiting years of work and/or hours of work. These limitations would result in the creation of jobs that in large part would be in the <u>private sector</u>. As shown in Chapters IX and X, the possible jobs created in this way would total more than 37 million.

| <u>Chapter</u> | <u>Action</u> | <u>Probable Employment Effect</u> (millions of jobs) |
|---|---|---|
| IX | Raise minimum work age | + 3.6 |
|  | National service | + 1.8 |
|  | Encourage early retirement | + 2.0 |
| X | Reduce working hours | <u>+ 30.0</u> |
| Total |  | + 37.4 |

Recommendations and Conclusions

This is well in excess of the 16 million additional jobs that Chapter VIII concluded would be required to reach full employment in 2005. In practice, some combination of limiting years of work and limiting hours of work would be most politically acceptable. The advantage of this approach is that private-sector jobs would not involve a burden on the taxpayer.

The previous chapters have recommended certain changes in present government policies that would increase the number of jobs over those that would be available in the absence of changes. Specifically, the following actions have been recommended.

## TAXES
Change payroll taxes and health-care financing to encourage employment, particularly in the service sector.
1. For all wages and salaries below $30,000 per year, eliminate payroll taxes. including Social Security, Medicare, workman's compensation, and unemployment insurance taxes. Adjust the rates on salaries above that figure (with no upper limit) to produce the same revenue as produced by the present taxes.
2. Finance health-care costs of all those with wages and salaries below $30,000 a year from a value-added tax on goods but not on services rather than from employer-paid insurance premiums based on the number of employees.
3. Continue present tax credits on industrial research.

## WAGES AND HOURS
1. Establish 35-hour workweek, with no reduction in salary, for all federal employees.
2. Over a period of five years, reduce the standard workweek for all businesses engaged in interstate commerce to 35 hours.

## CHAPTER XV

3. Adopt a universal calendar to give flexibility in future working-hour arrangements, such as the five-day weekend proposal discussed in Chapter X.

### EDUCATION
1. Increase funding for the Head Start program so that all eligible children can participate.
2. Raise the requirement for school attendance to age eighteen.
3. Adopt national performance standards for English, mathematics, and the sciences, with testing of all students in a nationally administered test.
4. Encourage apprenticeship programs.
5. Expand national service to encourage broad participation.

### RESEARCH
1. Increase government support for solar energy, particularly photovoltaic energy.
2. Establish new government-funded corporations to spur applied research in commercial products and processes.

### STRUCTURE AND INFRASTRUCTURE
1. Devise new government programs to encourage construction of low-cost housing.
2. Encourage high-speed intercity trains by passing legislation to provide for their operation on median strips of interstate highways.
3. Develop national standards for use in the transmission of data over "information highways."

### THE ARTS
1. Increase funding for the National Endowment for the Arts.
2. Establish paid positions of Poet Laureate, Artist Laureate, and Composer Laureate at all levels of government down to the county level.

## Recommendations and Conclusions

GOVERNMENT STATISTICS
1. Change the reported unemployment statistic to include those in part-time jobs who want to work full time and those who want jobs but are not actively seeking one.
2. Supplement the Gross National Product measurement with a composite index designed to measure Satisfaction of Human Needs.

Legislation to accomplish many of the above suggested actions has already been introduced in Congress. No concerted action has been taken, however, to group and press for the passage of all job-related legislation. <u>I suggest that the Vice President chair a Job Creation Task Force that would propose and expedite such legislation in a way similar to the effort that produced the 1993 report on Re-inventing Government.</u>

It was pointed out in the introductory chapter that in order to achieve full employment by the year 2005, the United States must add 40 million jobs from the base of 119 million jobs in 1993. The book has shown that this will be difficult but not impossible, particularly if some form of job sharing is adopted. The book also has shown that because of the current small size of the agricultural and manufacturing sectors in the U.S. economy, most of this job growth must come in the service sector, broadly defined. The tax changes proposed above would tend to tilt consumer demand away from goods toward services.

One common thread linking many of the diverse businesses in the service-producing sector is that a number of them directly or indirectly are involved in the "pursuit of happiness," which Thomas Jefferson listed in the Declaration of Independence along with life and liberty as one of the "unalienable rights" of humankind.[2] For instance, in order to be happy, one must be healthy. Education provided by the service sector increases the potential for happiness. The

## CHAPTER XV

travel, sports, and entertainment industries are directly linked to the pursuit of happiness. A recognition that Americans, after their basic needs are met, are searching for happiness would enable the government to shape its policies to meet public desires in ways more effective in creating jobs and less damaging to the environment than the present policies of maximizing employment through maximizing production of consumer goods. We no longer need more "bread" to meet the populace's desires. Certainly, however, there is room for more employment in those sectors of the economy such as health care, education, and "circuses" in the broad sense of amusements, which add to the sum total of human happiness. The potential for happiness also will be increased by providing more leisure rather than more goods.

Congress will act only if there is a groundswell of demand from the voters that national policy give priority to creating jobs rather than to maximizing the Gross National Product. Of course, the two are interrelated, but a program that emphasizes jobs, the environment, and the satisfaction of human needs, measured in ways suggested in the last chapter, will be quite different from past economic strategies that focused only on the growth of GNP. I hope that the readers of this book will lobby their representatives and senators to take the actions that will create the 40 million new jobs we need!

# APPENDIX A

# EMPLOYMENT AND INFLATION

*A*s pointed out in the Introduction, most U.S. economists believe that it would be impossible to achieve full employment as defined in this book (less than 3 percent unemployed) without at the same time producing an unacceptably high rate of inflation. Conventional theory holds that a certain level of unemployment is necessary for prices to be stable or to increase at an acceptably low rate. This is the "nonaccelerating inflation rate of unemployment" (NAIRU) discussed in the Introduction. In the United States, this minimum unemployment rate is considered to be between 5 and 7 percent, far above the desired 3 percent.

On the other hand, there have been periods both in the United States and abroad when a combination of low inflation and low unemployment existed. We shall examine the United States during the years 1948–1953 and Japan during 1981–1991.

## UNITED STATES

During the six-year period 1948–1953, the U.S. unemployment rate averaged 4.0 percent, varying between 2.9 and 3.3 percent in the last three years of that period. During that same period, the broadest measure of inflation, the implicit price deflator for the Gross National Product,

## APPENDIX A

rose by an average of 2.4 percent. and continued at about this level for the next ten years.[1]

Admittedly, the 1948–1953 period was an unusual one. By the second half of 1948, the pent-up demand released by the end of the Second World War had been satisfied, and a mild recession set in. Unemployment, which had averaged 3.8 percent in 1948, rose to an average of 5.9 percent in 1949. Although wages continued to rise, consumer prices actually fell. The recession was over by 1950, and the economy received a further boost by the outbreak of the Korean War in June 1950. Unemployment was only 3.3 percent in 1951 and 3.0 percent in 1952.[2]

The initial inflation resulting from wartime demand was dampened by government price and wage controls instituted by President Harry Truman in late 1950. Although administering these controls required 18,000 price and wage inspectors, they were effective. As noted above, even after the controls were removed by the Eisenhower administration in 1953, the average inflation rate for the next ten years was less than 3 percent. It was not full employment that ended this period of low inflation. It was the shock of the large increase in energy costs caused by the oil-price increases instigated by the OPEC cartel, compounded by increases in farm prices.

What this brief history seems to show is not that there is a causative relationship between unemployment and inflation but that both are responsive to the level of economic activity. When business is booming, firms both hire more people and try to raise their prices. During recessions, firms lay off employees and have more difficulty raising prices. The key is to achieve the desirable level of economic activity without inflation. One solution, that used by President Truman, is to institute price and wage controls. This experience shows that even after the controls are removed, the dampening of the inflationary expectations persists for years.

## Employment and Inflation

The economist Lester Thurow treated the inflationary phenomenon at some length in *The Zero-Sum Society.* He pointed out that there are three policies potentially available to governments to fight inflation: induce a recession through tight monetary policies, impose price and wage controls, or induce downward price shocks by such actions as abandoning agricultural price supports or changing the health-care system. Of government price and wage controls, Thurow wrote:

> The real objection to controls is not that they are cumbersome and inconvenient (they are) or that they won't work (they will), but that they must reduce someone's real income if they are to succeed in stopping inflation. It isn't possible to predict who this will be without knowing the exact details of any systems of controls, but there is no doubt that someone will be hurt. Some groups are vigorous opponents of controls because they believe that they will be the ones to suffer reduced incomes. Those groups that think they would gain under controls want controls.[3]

It is quite possible that some of the proposals to achieve full employment advocated in this book will lead labor leaders to press for higher wages, even in the absence of productivity gains or a rising cost of living. If this happens, it might be desirable again to impose price and wage controls for a few years until labor realizes that there is no basis for wage increases in their cost of living increases. A less drastic move would be to outlaw built-in cost-of-living increases in long-term labor contracts and eliminate them in government entitlement programs such as Social Security and government pensions. Either move would break the wage/price inflationary spiral and make continued high employment and low inflation more likely.

## APPENDIX A

### JAPAN

Since 1970, Japan's unemployment rate has fluctuated between 1.2 and 2.9 percent, averaging 2.5 percent in the last decade.[4] Nevertheless, this low unemployment rate was not achieved at the cost of high rates of inflation. Consumer prices in Japan between 1983 and 1988 rose at an average rate of only 1.1 percent.[5]

Japan is a democratic, capitalist country with a free-market economy. In detail, the economy differs from that of the United States in many ways, but the basic similarities of the two economies should allow us to learn from Japan in a way we never could have the socialist economies of the former Soviet Union and its allies, even if we had wanted to do so.

In terms of employment and unemployment, there are two significant differences between Japan and the United States. First, an employee in Japan tends to spend his or her whole working life with one firm. The employee has a vested interest in the firm, and the firm feels a strong responsibility for the employee. As one writer says, "He may not be fired for the trifling reason that the boss is losing money. If adjustments must be made, let the Old Man make them elsewhere."[6] Another writer points out that in Japan the attitudes of the workers are similar to those of the partners in a small-business venture in the United States, "who closely cooperate with each other because they share both the benefits and the costs of their joint business."[7] In this way, employees in Japan are isolated from the short-term swings in the business cycle. Most firms also continue to employ workers whose jobs have been eliminated by technological changes. This may be done temporarily by "make-work" jobs such as painting or gardening but often involves setting up a new subsidiary in an unrelated business and training the redundant employees as the workers in the new industry.

## Employment and Inflation

A second major difference between Japan and the United States is that in Japan most workers retire at age 55. Because this is the normal retirement age, those over 55 are not counted as unemployed. Employees are expected to provide for their retirement and do so through a very high rate of personal savings. By contrast, the United States in 1990 had more than 15 million workers age 55 and over.[8] As pointed out in Chapter IX, one way to reduce our unemployment would be to move toward the Japanese custom of retirement at age 55.

Japan has not had to resort to wage and price controls in order to prevent inflation in its full-employment economy. Rather, the natural inflationary tendency seems to have been controlled by careful monetary management, matching closely the growth of the money supply with the growth of the economy. In whatever way that the Japanese have done it, they have shown that it is possible to have full employment without inflation. This knowledge alone should encourage our Federal Reserve to attempt to match Japan's achievement.

# SOURCES AND NOTES

**CHAPTER I: INTRODUCTION**
1. *Business Statistics 1963–91*, U.S. Department of Commerce, Bureau of Economic Analysis (Washington, DC: U.S. Government Printing Office, 1992) pp.45-47.
2. A detailed discussion of theories relating to the motivation to work can be found in:
David Macarov, *Incentives to Work* (San Francisco: Jossey-Bass, 1976) pp.61-107.
3. *Employment and Earnings*, U.S. Department of Labor, Bureau of Labor Statistics, (January 1993), Table 35, p.214.
4. Ibid., Table 31, p.211.
5. *Statistical Abstract of the United States, 1993*, U.S. Department of Commerce, Bureau of the Census (Washington, DC: U.S. Government Printing Office, 1993) Table 1403, p.859.
6. *New York Times* (May 26, 1992), p.D3. (The *Times*'s source is given as the Organization for Economic Cooperation and Development (OECD) and the Gerrman Institute for Economics.)
7. Howard N. Fullerton, Jr., "Another Look at the Labor Force," *Monthly Labor Review* (November 1993), pp.31-34. The projection is based on both the natural increase in the population and a forecasted net immigration of 880,000 between 1992 and 2005. Of the 24 million increase in the

113

## FULL EMPLOYMENT

work force, 14 million are forecast to be women, whose labor participation rate is expected to increase from 58 to 63 percent.

8. This figure is derived from the U.S. merchandise trade deficit in 1991 of $76.8 billion. (*Survey of Current Business*, June, 1993, p.11.) Since this is about 4.0 percent of the total value of U.S. goods in 1991 of $1.9 trillion (*Business Statistics 1963-1991*, Appendix II, p.A-101), the effect on the total manufacturing employment in 1991 of 18.4 million people (*Monthly Labor Review*, September 1993) would be about 740,000. Actually, the effect is probably less, since incremental foreign trade would primarily effect blue-collar manufacturing workers, which numbered only 12.5 million.

9. *Statistical Abstract, 1993*, Table 648, p.410, "Motor Vehicles and Equipment." The figure for 1975 was 792,000 and for 1990 was 809,000.

10. Paul Krugman, *The Age of Diminished Expectations: U.S. Economic Policy in the 1990's* (Cambridge, MA: The M.I.T. Press, 1990), p.29.

11. *Historical Statistics of the United States*, U.S. Department of Commerce, Bureau of the Census (Washington, DC: U.S. Government Printing Office, 1975). The inflation figures are taken from Series E 1-22, p.197, "Implicit Price Deflators for the Gross National Product," with the 1947 figure 74.6 and the 1953 figure 88.3; 2.4 percent is the geometric average. The unemployment figures are from Series D 85-86, p.135, and are the numerical average for the seven years. The 1947 figure was 3.9 percent and the 1953 figure was 2.9 percent, with no obvious trend in between.

12. *Statistical Abstract, 1993*, Tables 1401 and 1403, pp.858-859. Since 1970, Japan's unemployment rate has never exceeded 3 percent, but this has not resulted in high inflation. (An article in the November 28, 1993, issue of *The New York Times*, pp.1,20, points out that the Japanese unemployment rate of 2.6 percent in the latter half of 1993 did not include women who were layed off and decided not

## SOURCES AND NOTES

to seek another job. U.S. statistics, however, do not include those who have dropped out of the labor force, either.)
13. Eamonn Fingleton, "Fine, Thank You," *Atlantic Monthly* (May 1993), p.24. Fingleton is an economic journalist who has lived in Japan since 1985.

**CHAPTER II: EMPLOYMENT IN MANUFACTURING**
1. *Business Statistics 1963-91*, Appendix II, pp.A-96-97.
2. *New York Times* (March 9, 1986), p.1.
3. *Business Statistics 1963-1991*, p.47(employment) and A-97 (expenditures).
4. *Business Statistics 1963-91,* pp.45-46.
5. 1979 figures are from *National Income and Product Accounts 1959-1988* (U.S. Department of Commerce, 1992), table 4.4, p.170. 1991 figures are from *Survey of Current Business* (U.S. Department of Commerce, June 1993), Table 4.4, p.11. The table in the text omits the category "foods, feeds, and beverages," which in part are consumer products and had a favorable trade balance each year, but it does include in the "automotive vehicles, engines and parts" category automotive vehicles for industrial and government use, which had an unfavorable balance. These two tend to cancel each other out.
6. Robert W. Bednarzik, "An Analysis of U.S. Industries Sensitive to Foreign Trade: 1982-1987*,"* *Monthly Labor Review* (February, 1993), pp.15-29.
7. *Statistical Abstract, 1993*, Table No. 664, p.423.
8. Kurt Vonnegut, *Player Piano* (New York: Delacorte Press, 1952.)
9. Otis Port, with John Carey, Kevin Kelly, and Stephanie Anderson Forest, "Quality," *Business Week* (November 30, 1992), pp.66-74.
10. Al Ehrbar, "Price of Progress: Re-Engineering Gives Firms New Efficiency, Workers the Pink Slip," *Wall Street Journal* (March 16, 1993), pp.A1, A11.

FULL EMPLOYMENT

11. James C. Franklin, "Industry Output and Employment," *Monthly Labor Review* (November 1993), Table 5, p.52. The article gives three different projections for the year 2005. The 500,000 job loss is in their "moderate" scenario. The "low-growth" scenario would lead to a 2.1 million job loss in manufacturing between 1992 and 2005 and the "high" scenario forecasts an 800,000 job gain.
12 Thorstein Veblen, *The Theory of the Leisure Class*, Modern Library (New York: Random House, 1934).
13. John Kenneth Galbraith, *The Affluent Society* (Boston, MA: Houghton Mifflin, 1958), pp.355-56.

**CHAPTER III: EMPLOYMENT IN SERVICES**
1. *Business Statistics 1963-1991*, Appen. II, pp.A-97, A-101.
2. Ibid. p.47.
3. Al Ehrbar, "Price of Progress: Re-Engineering Gives Firms New Efficiency, Workers the Pink Slip", *Wall Street Journal* (March 16, 1993), pp.A1, A11.
4. David R. Hiles, "Health Services: The Real Job Machine," *Monthly Labor Review* (November 1992), pp.3-16.
5. James C. Franklin, "Industry Output and Employment, *Monthly Labor Review* (November 1993), pp.41-55.
6. Juvenal, *Satire X*, line 80. The Latin is, *Duas tantum res anxius optat, Panem et circenses*. From John Bartlett, *Familiar Quotations*, Thirteenth Edition, p.63.
7. Tom McNichol and Gayle Jo Ayala, "Mountains of Cash," *USA TODAY* (March 20, 1992), Magazine, pp.4-5.
8. Umberto Eco, *Travels in Hyperreality* (New York: Harcourt Brace Jovanovich, 1986).
9. Franklin, op.cit.
10. Ibid.
11. Ibid.

# SOURCES AND NOTES

## CHAPTER IV: EMPLOYMENT FROM TECHNOLOGY
1. *Statistical Abstract, 1993*, Table 973, p.595. Although defense expenditures were about two-thirds of <u>federal</u> research and development costs, they were only about one-third of total national costs, including universities and industry.
2. Shawn Carlson, "Slaves to *Freedom*," *The Humanist* (January/February 1992), pp.5-10, 36.
3. Faye Flam, "The SSC: Radical Therapy for Physics," *Science* (October 11, 1991), pp.194-96.
4. David P. Hamilton, "Lightning Strikes the SSC", *Science* (June 26, 1992), pp.1752-53.
5. Edward Edelson, "Solar Cell Update," *Popular Science* (June 1992), pp.95-99.
6. Joan O'C. Hamilton, "Virtual Reality: How a Computer-Generated World Could Change the Real World," *Business Week* (October 5, 1992), pp.97-105.
7. Steve Ditlea, "Space: Computerized Tour Guides," *Omni* (October 1990), p.26.
8. Shawn Carlson, "Virtual Mars?", *The Humanist* (March/April 1991), pp.43-45.
9. Don E. Kash and Robert W. Rycroft, "Nurturing Winners with Federal R&D," *Technology Review* (November/December 1993), pp.59-66.
10. "Wanted: A Defense R&D Policy," *Scientific American* (December 1993), pp.47-50.

## CHAPTER V: EMPLOYMENT FROM STRUCTURE AND INFRASTRUCTURE
1. *Business Statistics 1963-91*, p.45.
2. *Statistical Abstract, 1993*, Table 1211, p.713. The source is given as the Bureau of Census publication *Census of Construction Industries, 1987.*
3. Nancy Reder, "The Search for Low-Cost Housing," *National Voter* (August 1988), p.5.
4. *Statistical Abstract, 1993*, Table 1219, p.717.

FULL EMPLOYMENT

5. Peter Coy and Neil Gross, "The Highway to Tomorrow," *Business Week* (October 23, 1992), p.200.
6. Jerry Gray, "New Jersey Bell Wins Approval for Fiber Optics," *New York Times* (December 23, 1992), p.1.
7. Richard Zoglin, "Beyond Your Wildest Dreams", *Time* (Vol,140. Issue 27, Fall 1992), p.70.
8. G. Freeman Allen, *Railways: Past, Present, and Future* (New York: William Morrow, 1982), p.289.
9. Joseph Vranich, *Super-Trains: Solutions to America's Transportation Gridlock* (New York: St. Martin's Press, 1991).
10. David Scott and John Free, "310-mph Flying Trains—in the 90's—in the U.S.," *Popular Science* (May, 1989), pp.132-136, 159.
11. Jeff Plungis, "The Next Transportation Revolution," *Empire State Report* (September 1993), pp.37-38.

**CHAPTER VI: EMPLOYMENT IN GOVERNMENT**
1. *Historical Statistics of the United States* (White Plains, NY: Kraus International, 1989), pp.126, 137.
2. *Business Statistics 1963-1991*, p.47.
3. *Statistical Abstract, 1993*, Table 500, p.318.
4. James C. Franklin, "Industry Output and Employment," *Monthly Labor Review* (November, 1993), p.56.

**CHAPTER VII: EMPLOYMENT FROM CREATIVITY**
1. Robert Redfield, "How Human Society Operates," in *Man, Culture, and Society*, Harry L. Shapiro, ed., (New York: Oxford University Press, 1960), p.366.
2. *Occupational Outlook Handbook 1992-1993*, U.S. Department of Labor (Washington, DC: U.S. Government Printing Office, 1992).
3. James Vinson and D.L. Kilpatrick, eds., *Contemporary Poets, Contemporary Novelists, Contemporary Dramatists* (New York: St. Martin's Press, 1985-1988).

## SOURCES AND NOTES

4. Herbert Muschamp, "When Art Becomes a Public Spectacle," *New York Times* (August 29, 1993), Sect.2, p.1.

**CHAPTER VIII: RECAPITULATION**
1. *Business Week* (February 22, 1993), p.71. The source of data is given as Lowell Gallaway.
2. *Statistical Abstract, 1993*, Table 528, p.341.
3. Ibid.
4. Bradley R. Braden and Stephanie L. Hyland, "Cost of Employee Compensation in Public and Private Sectors," *Monthly Labor Review* (May 1993), p.15. $1.02 per hour is the cost for private industry.
5, *Economic Report to the President*, Council of Economic Advisors, (Washington, DC: U.S. Government Printing Office, January 1993). Table B-2, p.350.

**CHAPTER IX: LIMITING YEARS OF WORK**
1. Howard W. Fullerton, Jr., "Labor Force Projection," *Monthly Labor Review* (November 1991), pp.31-44.
2. *Statistical Abstract, 1993,* Table No. 639, p.402.
3. Ibid., Table 622, p.393.
4. William James, "The Moral Equivalent of War." This was an address given at Stanford University on February 25, 1906. It was first printed in *McClure's Magazine* (August 1910). A current source is in *The Moral Equivalent of War and Other Essays* and *Selections from Some Problems in Philosophy*, John K. Roth, ed. (New York: Harper & Row), pp.3-16.
5. Charles C. Moskos, *A Call to Civic Service: National Service for Country and Community* (New York: The Free Press), 1988, pp.145-165.
6. Richard Danzig and Peter Szanton, *National Service: What Would It Mean?* (Lexington, MA: Lexington Books, 1986).
7. Fullerton, op.cit.

FULL EMPLOYMENT

**CHAPTER X: LIMITING HOURS OF WORK**
1. A good history of the labor movements for the eight-hour day and forty-hour workweek can be found in:
Thomas R. Brooks, *Toil and Trouble: A History of American Labor* (New York: Delacorte Press, 1971).
2. Ferdinand Protzman, "German Companies Finding Low-Cost Locations in U.S." *The New York Times* (May 26, 1992), pp.D1, D3. The source is listed as the Organization for Economic Cooperation and Development, German Institute for Economics.
3. *New York Times* (November 22, 1993), pp.A1, A6.
4. Benjamin Kline Hunnicutt, *Work Without End: Abandoning Shorter Hours for the Right to Work* (Philadelphia: Temple University Press, 1988), p.311.
5. *New York Times* (May 16, 1993), p.18.
6. *New York Times* (June 3, 1990), "This Week in Review," Sect.4, p.1,3.
7. Peter Kilborn, "Labor Wants Shorter Hours To Make Up for Job Losses," *New York Times* (October 11, 1993), p.A-10.
8. Peter M Rinaldo, *The Five-Day Weekend: A Proposal for Calendar and Work-Schedule Change* (Briarcliff Manor, NY: DorPete Press, 1989). Readers who wish to find out details of this proposal may obtain a free paperback copy (while supplies last) by sending $1.00 for postage to DorPete Press, P.O. Box 238, Briarcliff Manor, NY 10510.

**CHAPTER XI: CONQUERING THE FEAR OF LEISURE**
1. Mihaly Csikszentmihalyi, "Relax? Relax and Do What?," *New York Times* (August 12, 1993), p.A25.
2. John A. Ryan, "High Wages and Unemployment," *Commonweal* (January 7, 1931), p.260.
3. Hunnicutt, op.cit., p.99
4. Ibid., p.104
5. William Bennett, *Wall Street Journal* (March 15, 1993).

## SOURCES AND NOTES

6. Dorothy Canfield Fisher, "The Bright Perilous Face of Leisure," *Newsletter—Society For The Reduction Of Human Labor* (Spring 1993), vol.3, no.2, Reprinted from *The Journal of Adult Education* originally published in "the early '30's."
7. The song "Are You Havin' any Fun?" was written by lyricist Sammy Fain and composer Jack Yellin for the revue *George White's Scandals of 1939.* It was later recorded by the singer Ella Logan and Tommy Dorsey's orchestra. It is quoted by permission of Warner Chappell, the copyright owner.

## CHAPTER XII: FIRST PRECONDITION FOR FULL EMPLOYMENT

1. Elizabeth Neuffer, "Poor Skills Cited in New York Entry-Level Applicants," *New York Times* (July 4, 1987), pp.29,31.
2. Hudson Institute, *Workforce 2000* (U.S. Government Printing Office, 1987), p.88.
3. *USA TODAY* (June 8, 1992), p.B-4.
4. *Statistical Abstract, 1993*, Table 264, p.169.
5. Steven Greenhouse, "If the French Can Do It, Why Can't We?" *New York Times Magazine* (November 14, 1993), pp.59-62.
6. Judith Weiss, "News on Science Education," *Bioscience* (December 1989), p.763.
7. William Celis, 3rd, "International Report Card Shows U.S. Schools Work," *New York Times* (December 9, 1993), pp.1,26.
8. *New York Times* (March 3, 1990), p.A-22.
9. William Celis, 3rd, "The Fight Over National Standards," *New York Times* (August 1, 1993), Sect. 4A, pp.14-16.
10. Edward N. Luttwak, *The Endangered American Dream*," (New York: Simon & Schuster, 1993).
11. M.J. Barnett, "The Case for More School Days," *The Atlantic* (November 1990), pp.78-106.

FULL EMPLOYMENT

12. Margaret Hilton, "Shared Training: Learning from Germany," *Monthly Labor Review* (March 1991), pp.33-37.
13. National Center on Education and the Economy, *America's Choice: High Skills or Low Wages!*, (Rochester, NY: National Center, 1990).
   This book is a report of the Commission on the Skills of the American Workforce. The commission was chaired by Ira Magaziner, who went on to become chairman of Hillary Rodham Clinton's health care task force.
14. William Celis, 3rd, "Study Shows Half of Adults in U.S. Can't Read or Handle Arithmetic," *The New York Times* (September 9, 1993), pp.A1, A22.

## CHAPTER XIII: SECOND PRECONDITIUON FOR FULL EMPLOYMENT

1. Paul Samuelson, *Economics: An Introductory Analysis,*- sixth ed. (New York: McGraw-Hill, 1964), pp.340-41.
2. Paul Samuelson and William Nordhaus, *Economics*, 12th ed. (New York: McGraw-Hill, 1985), pp.366=67.
3. A.W. Phillips, "The Relation Between Unemployment and the Rate of Change of Money Wage Rates in the United Kingdom, 1861-1957," *Economics* 25 (1958), pp.283-99.
4. Paul Krugman, *The Age of Diminished Expectations: U.S. Economic Policy in the 1990's* (Cambridge, MA: The M.I.T. Press, 1990), p.29.
5. Robert Heilbroner and Lester Thurow, *Economics Explained* (Englewood Cliffs, NJ: Prentice-Hall, 1982), pp.63-69.
6. *Survey of Current Business* (June 1993), U.S. Dept. of Commerce, Table 4.1, p.11.
7. *Historical Statistics of the United States,* U.S. Department of Commerce (1976), Series E 1-22, p.197.
8. Heilbroner and Thurow, op.cit., pp.93-98.
9. Samuelson and Nordhaus, op.cit., p.358.
10. Paul Krugman, op.cit., p.29.

## SOURCES AND NOTES

11. George P. Brockway, *Economics: What Went Wrong and Why and Some Things to Do About It* (New York: Harper & Row, 1985), p.166.
12. *Statistical Abstract, 1993*, Table 1403, p.859.
13. Karen Rothmeyer, "Bloated Pay," *Mother Jones* (July/-August, 1992), pp.23-24.
14, Sam Pizzigati, *The Maximum Wage* (New York: Apex Press, 1992).

**CHAPTER XIV: THE GREAT GOD G.N.P.**
1. *Business Statistics 1963-91*, "Methodological Notes for Appendix II."
2. Victor Anderson, *Alternative Economic Indicators* (New York: Routledge, 1991), pp.22=23.
3. *Business Statistics 1963-1991*, Appendix II, p.A-102.
4. *Handbook of Labor Statistics - 1988*, U.S. Department of Labor, Bureau of Labor Statistics (U.S. Government Printing Office, 1989), Table 12, p.54.
5. Ibid., Table 100, pp.356-57.
6. Victor Anderson, op.cit.

**CHAPTER XV — RECOMMENDATIONS AND CONCLUSIONS**
1. Lester Thurow, *The Zero-Sum Society* (New York: Basic Books, 1980), pp.203-4.
2. Thomas Jefferson, Declaration of Independence, July 4, 1776. Bartlett's *Familiar Quotations* points out that this phrase of the Declaration is often misquoted as "inalienable."

**APPENDIX A: EMPLOYMENT AND INFLATION**
1. The statistics quoted in this and the following paragraph are from:
*Historical Statistics of the United States*, U.S. Department of Commerce (1976).
2. Charles Hession and Sardy Hyman, *Ascent to Affluence: A History of American Economic Deveopment* (Boston: Allyn and Bacon, 1969), pp. 807-11.

FULL EMPLOYMENT

3. Lester Thurow, pp.41-76.
4. *Statistical Abstract, 1993*, Table 1403, p.859.
5. *The Economist Book of Vital World Statistics* (New York: Random House, 1990), p.144.
6. Burton Crane, *The Practical Economist* (New York: Simon and Schuster, 1960), pp.111-112.
7. Robert Ozaki, *Human Capitalism* (New York: Kodansha International, 1991), p.93.
8. *Statistical Abstract ,1993,* Table 622, p.393.

# INDEX

Advertising, 13-24
Agricultural employment, 1,48
Amtrak, 45
Amusements and recreation, 29-31
Anderson, Victor, 99
Apprenticeship programs, 83,104
Artists, 9,53-54
Automotive industry, 6
Balance of trade, 5,6, 17-19,88
Bell Atlantic, 44
Bennett, William, 76
Blue-collar workers, 1,16
Brazil
 debt, 90
 income distribution, 92
Bureau of Labor Statistics, 3,5
Bush, Pres. George, 82
Business services, 29
Calendar, universal, 73,104
Canada, health-care costs, 57
Carlson, Shawn, 40
Carter, Pres. Jimmy, 65, 67
Celebrity incomes, 31
Choreographers, 54
Clinton, Pres. Bill, 82
Construction Industry, 42-43
Consumer goods, 8,12-24
Consumer services, 8,25-34
Conyers. Rep. John, 71
Creative arts, 52-55
Dancers, 54

Danzig, Richard, 66
Declaration of Independence, 105
Deficit, federal, 90
Deming, W. Edwards, 21
DRI/McGraw Hill, 44
Education, 8,80-84,104
Education Act of 1993, 84
Education employment, 49-50
Eisenhower, Pres. Dwight, 108
Exchange rate, effect on employment, 6
Financial services, 29
Fisher, Dorothy Canfield, 76,78
*Five-Day Weekend*, 72-74
Food service, 29
France
 child care, 80-81
 education, 82
 intercity trains, 45
 working hours, 70
Freeman, Richard, 72
Friedman, Milton, 7
Full employment, definition, 3-4
Galbraith, John Kenneth, 23
Gambling, 30
General Agreement on Tariffs and Trade (GATT), 88
Germany
 education, 82
 intercity trains, 45
 wages, 70
 working hours, 4,70

125

# FULL EMPLOYMENT

Gore, Albert, 39,105
Government employment
  federal, 48-51
  local, 48-51
  state, 48-51
Greece, 2,52
Gross National Product,
  11,87-88,91-100,105
Gross Domestic Product, 94
Habitat for Humanity, 67
Head Start, 81,104
Health care, 28-29, 50
Heilbroner, Robert, 93
Helmsley, Leona, 23
Hours of work, 69-74
Housing, 42-43,104
Hudson Institute, 80
Imports, effect on
  employment, 17-19
Income distribution, 3,90-92
Inflation, 7,87,89,107-111
Information highways,
  44-45,104
Infrastructure, 9,44-47
James, William, 64-65
Japan
  education, 82
  income distribution, 91-92
  inflation, 7,110
  intercity trains, 45
  retirement age, 67
  unemployment rate,
  4,7,110-111
Jefferson, Thomas, 105
Johnson, Pres. Lyndon, 65
Juvenal, 29
Kash, Don E., 40
Kennedy, Pres. John F., 65

Krugman, Paul, 90
Kutscher, Robert E., 72
Larrouturou, Pierre, 70-71
Lawrence Livermore
  Laboratory, 40
Leacock, Stephen, 76
Leisure, 10,32,75-80
Los Alamos Laboratory, 40
Luddites, 34
Luttwak, Edward, 82
Maglev trains, 46-47
Malcolm Baldridge Award,
  22
Manufacturing Employment,
  12-24
Marcos, Imelda, 13,22
Marshall, Alfred, 86
*Maximum Wage*, 92-93
McGuire, Peter, 69
Mexico, debt, 90
Mill, John Stuart, 86
Moskos, Charles C., 65-66
Moynihan, Sen. Patrick, 47
NAFTA, 88
NASA, 36,40
NAIRU, 7,87,107
National Endowment for the
  Arts, 54,104
National Urban League, 80
National youth corps,
  64-67,104
New Deal. 79
New Jersey Bell, 44
New York Telephone, 79
Nonaccelerating inflation
  rate of unemployment
  (NAIRU), 7,87,107
Nordhaus, William, 90,93

## FULL EMPLOYMENT

(NAIRU), 7,87,107
Nordhaus, William, 90,93
North American Free Trade Agreement (NAFTA), 88
Olympic Games, 52,55
OPEC cartel, 108
Phillips, A.C., 87
Phillips Curve, 87
Phoenix, Arizona, 55
Photographers, 54
Photovoltaic energy, 36-37
Pigou, A.C., 86
Price controls, 108-109
Productivity, 19
PVUSA, 37
Re-engineering, 22,27-28
Redfield, Robert, 52
Research and development, 24,35-41,104
Ricardo, David, 86
Roosevelt, Pres. Franklin D., 65
Ryan, John A., 75
Rycroft, Robert W., 40
Samuelson, Paul, 86,90,02
Satisfaction of Human Needs, 99-100,105
Say's Law, 86
Schooling, mandatory, 64
Schor, Juliet B. 72
Service-producing sector, 25-34
Shingo Prize, 22
Shopping, 31
Silver, Abba Hillel, 76
Social Security, 57-58, 60
Sound economy, 8,85-93
South Korea, education, 82
Space Station *Freedom*, 36-37
Sports, 30
Structures, 9
Student Conservation Association, 66
Super-Conducting Super Collider, 37
Sweden
 unemployment rate, 4
 income distribution, 91-92
Szanton, Peter, 66
Taxes
 payroll, 11,57-59,103
 value-added, 11,59-62,103
Television, 30
Thurow, Lester, 93,101, 109
Total Quality Management, 21-22
Trade, balance of, 5,6, 17-19,88
Trains,
 intercity, 45-47,104
 maglev, 46-47
Truman, Pres. Harry. 65, 108
Trump, Donald and Ivana, 22
Unemployment, negative effects, 2
Unemployment statistics
 discouraged workers, 3
 part-time workers, 3
Veblen, Thorstein, 23
Virtual reality, 38-40
Vonnegut, Kurt, 20
Wilson, Pres. Woodrow, 65
Work force, composition by age, 63

127

## FULL EMPLOYMENT

Work, motivation for, 2
Working hours, reduction of,
 4,9,11,69-74,103
Workweek, 69-74,103
WPA, 102
Writers, 9,53
Youth Corps, 64-67,104
*Zero-Sum Society,* 101,109